A Catholic Handbook for
ENGAGED
and
NEWLY MARRIED
COUPLES

by Frederick W. Marks, Ph.D.

EMMAUS
ROAD
PUBLISHING

To Mary Anne

A Catholic Handbook for
ENGAGED
and
NEWLY MARRIED
COUPLES

by Frederick W. Marks, Ph.D.

EMMAUS
ROAD
PUBLISHING

Nihil Obstat
Rev. James Dunfee
Censor Librorum

Imprimatur ✠
Most Rev. Gilbert I. Sheldon, D.D., D.Min.
Bishop of Steubenville

Nihil Obstat
Rev. Jonathan Morse, Ph.D.
Censor

Imprimatur ✠
Most Rev. Basil H. Losten
Bishop of Stamford (Ukrainian Rite)

Copyright © 2001
Emmaus Road Publishing
All rights reserved.
10 09 08   3 4

Library of Congress catalog no. 94-072069

Published by
Emmaus Road Publishing
a division of Catholics United for the Faith
827 North Fourth Street
Steubenville, Ohio 43952
(800) 398-5470

Cover design and layout by
Beth Hart

The cover art is Bartolomeo Murillo's
Holy Family with Sparrow, located in the
Museo del Prado, Madrid, Spain. Used with
permission of Scala/Art Resource, New York.

Published in the United States of America
ISBN 1-931018-01-4
ISBN 13: 978-1-931018-01-2

Contents

≈ Acknowledgments ≈

I should like to thank the following persons for taking the time to read rough drafts of this handbook and for offering valuable suggestions: Fr. Kenneth Baker, S.J.; Fr. Avery Dulles, S.J.; Very Rev. Peter M.J. Stravinskas; Rev. Robert D. Smith; Fr. James Torrens, S.J.; Rev. C. John McCloskey III; Drs. Raúl and Liliana Alessandri; Dave and Phyllis Burns; Anne Carroll; Patricia Pucetti; Dr. Michael Karol; Mary Frances Lester; John Metzler; the late Bill and Frances Reck, along with their daughter, Mary Ann; Laurie Balbach Taylor; Leon Suprenant and his staff at Emmaus Road Publishing; and last but not least, my wife, Sylvia, sweetheart and best friend for over thirty-five years, who contributed in every way imaginable.

Author's Preface to the Second Edition

There are few changes in this edition of the *Catholic Handbook*. The sections on abortion, divorce, and annulment have been strengthened, and a detailed outline of the case against contraception has been added. Aside from this, however, the text remains substantially the same.

Readers will continue to find in the appendices a set of powerful tools to reinforce their knowledge of the faith, along with their ability to defend it. The comprehensive questionnaire for engaged couples at the end of the book is designed to stimulate discussion and facilitate an honest assessment of differences prior to the wedding. But it may also be useful at a later date to take stock of where one stands and to readjust the long-term compass.

From true love springs an enormous power for good, and the more questions one raises, the greater the likelihood of a smooth transition to married life. May this be the beginning of a joyous and fruitful journey, and may it end for each and every one of us in the arms of God.

Frederick W. Marks, Ph.D.
December 2000

⚘ Abbreviations ⚘

The Old Testament
Gen./Genesis
Ex./Exodus
Lev./Leviticus
Num./Numbers
Deut./Deuteronomy
Josh./Joshua
Judg./Judges
Ruth/Ruth
1 Sam./1 Samuel
2 Sam./2 Samuel
1 Kings/1 Kings
2 Kings/2 Kings
1 Chron./1 Chronicles
2 Chron./2 Chronicles
Ezra/Ezra
Neh./Nehemiah
Tob./Tobit
Jud./Judith
Esther/Esther
Job/Job
Ps./Psalms
Prov./Proverbs
Eccles./Ecclesiastes
Song/Song of Solomon
Wis./Wisdom
Sir./Sirach (Ecclesiasticus)
Is./Isaiah
Jer./Jeremiah
Lam./Lamentations

Bar./Baruch
Ezek./Ezekiel
Dan./Daniel
Hos./Hosea
Joel/Joel
Amos/Amos
Obad./Obadiah
Jon./Jonah
Mic./Micah
Nahum/Nahum
Hab./Habakkuk
Zeph./Zephaniah
Hag./Haggai
Zech./Zechariah
Mal./Malachi
1 Mac./1 Maccabees
2 Mac./2 Maccabees

The New Testament
Mt./Matthew
Mk./Mark
Lk./Luke
Jn./John
Acts/Acts of the Apostles
Rom./Romans
1 Cor./1 Corinthians
2 Cor./2 Corinthians
Gal./Galatians
Eph./Ephesians
Phil./Philippians

Col./Colossians	Jas./James
1 Thess./1 Thessalonians	1 Pet./1 Peter
2 Thess./2 Thessalonians	2 Pet./2 Peter
1 Tim./1 Timothy	1 Jn./1 John
2 Tim./2 Timothy	2 Jn./2 John
Tit./Titus	3 Jn./3 John
Philem./Philemon	Jude/Jude
Heb./Hebrews	Rev./Revelation (Apocalypse)

Scripture Copyright

Unless otherwise indicated, Scripture quotations are taken from the Revised Standard Version, Catholic Edition (RSVCE), copyright © 1965 and 1966 by the Division of Christian Education of the National Council of the Churches of Christ in the United States of America. Used by permission.

Catechism of the Catholic Church

Throughout the text, the *Catechism of the Catholic Church* (United States Catholic Conference–Libreria Editrice Vaticana, 1994, as revised in the 1997 Latin typical edition) will be cited simply as "Catechism."

Catechism Copyright

Excerpts from the Catechism are taken from the English translation of the *Catechism of the Catholic Church* for the United States of America copyright © 1994/1997, United States Catholic Conference—Libreria Editrice Vaticana. All rights reserved.

Code of Canon Law

All quotations from the current (1983) Code of Canon Law are taken from *Code of Canon Law, Latin-English Edition*, Washington: Canon Law Society of America, copyright © 1983. Throughout the text, passages from the 1983 Code will be cited simply by reference to "canon."

Documents of Vatican II

SC Constitution on the Sacred Liturgy (*Sacrosanctum Concilium*), December 4, 1963

IM Decree on the Means of Social Communication (*Inter Mirifica*), December 4, 1963

LG Dogmatic Constitution on the Church (*Lumen Gentium*), November 21, 1964

OE Decree on the Catholic Eastern Churches (*Orientalium Ecclesiarum*), November 21, 1964

UR Decree on Ecumenism (*Unitatis Redintegratio*), November 21, 1964

CD Decree on the Pastoral Office of Bishops in the Church (*Christus Dominus*), October 28, 1965

PC Decree on the Up-to-Date Renewal of Religious Life (*Perfectae Caritatis*), October 28, 1965

OT Decree on the Training of Priests (*Optatam Totius*), October 28, 1965

GE Declaration on Christian Education (*Gravissimum Educationis*), October 28, 1965

NA Declaration on the Relation of the Church to Non-Christian Religions (*Nostra Aetate*), October 28, 1965

DV Dogmatic Constitution on Divine Revelation (*Dei Verbum*), November 18, 1965

AA Decree on the Apostolate of Lay People (*Apostolicam Actuositatem*), November 18, 1965

DH   Declaration on Religious Liberty
(*Dignitatis Humanae*), December 7, 1965

AG   Decree on the Church's Missionary Activity
(*Ad Gentes Divinitus*), December 7, 1965

PO   Decree on the Ministry and Life of Priests
(*Presbyterorum Ordinis*), December 7, 1965

GS   Pastoral Constitution on the Church in the Modern
World (*Gaudium et Spes*), December 7, 1965

⁓ Foreword ⁓

It is not easy to find authentically Catholic books and pamphlets to help engaged and newly married couples. Unfortunately, many of them are defective, either because they reject important aspects of Catholic teaching on marriage and family life, or because they simply omit things the authors do not agree with, such as the immorality of artificial birth control. There are no such problems with Dr. Frederick Marks' brief *Catholic Handbook*.

This handbook is outstanding both for its practicality and for its fidelity to the Catholic faith. It is practical because it offers good suggestions on most aspects of married life, such as the wedding, the honeymoon, the relationship between husband and wife, in-laws, finances, raising children, sexual relations, practicing the faith, and developing a spiritual life of personal relations with God.

The handbook is also thoroughly Catholic. It offers excellent advice on how to live the Catholic faith as a married man or woman. There is no waffling here, no dissent, no ambiguity. The author spells out clearly what the Catholic Church expects of married people in the areas of married life, sexuality, and family life.

Of course, there is no such thing as a "quick fix" or an easy solution to the difficulties to be faced by any man and woman who commit themselves to each other for life. It is not easy for any two people to live together day in and day out without some disagreement and friction. But Dr. Marks gives engaged and newly married couples some advance warnings on what to expect and, even more importantly, he offers some sage advice on how to deal with problems—advice which is based on his own experience and on the accumulated wisdom of the Catholic Church.

So if you are looking for some help to make your Catholic marriage the best it can possibly be, in my opinion you will be amply rewarded by a careful reading and reflection on the handbook and by having a frank discussion of it with your spouse.

Father Kenneth Baker, S.J.

⁀ Chapter 1 ⁀
Introduction to Matrimony

Marriage is like a fine wine; it improves with age and appreciates in value. Torrents of worries and difficulties are incapable of drowning true love because people who sacrifice themselves generously are brought closer together in the long run. . .

Blessed Josemaría Escrivá de Balaguer

Never be cynical about love, for in the face of all aridity and disenchantment, it is as perennial as the grass. . .

Max Ehrmann

There is nothing in the world—no possible success, military or political, which is worth weighing in the balance for one moment against the happiness that comes to those fortunate enough to make a real love match—a match in which lover and sweetheart will never be lost in husband and wife. I know what I am writing about, for I am just as much devoted to Mrs. Roosevelt now as ever I was. . .

Theodore Roosevelt
President of the United States (1901-09)
at the age of forty

What Do You Think of Marriage?

Marriage has been variously described as a great work, a great adventure, a great responsibility, and a great joy. Needless to say, it is all of these, not to mention a great disappointment to those who approach it irreverently or ill prepared. But above all, marriage is a great vocation, full of grace for those who give to it all that they are and possess. Scripture tells us that Jesus blessed the wedding feast at Cana with a sudden burst of spiritual energy, nothing less than His first public miracle. Surely, He must have thought the occasion a worthy one.[1] My parents used to say that although their life together was not always smooth sailing—they had their share of arguments—it was nonetheless worth it. And so it was. Have you ever known anyone to be unhappy who was happily married? Many, on the other hand, with successful careers and a high standard of living, feel emotionally devastated because they are insecure at home or because their marriage has crashed. The right partner will bring out the best in you, soothing your heart when it aches and tapping hidden strengths—in short, helping you to make of the "lumber of your life not a tavern, but a temple." You, in turn, will do the same for your better half, just as the two of you, working together, will afford solace and comfort to friends and neighbors by the warmth of your hospitality.

The other side of the coin is that the same spouse who soothes will also irritate, tempting you at times to commit everything short of hari-kari. Marriage multiplies responsibilities and puts one to the test in unforeseen ways. If, based on what you are able to observe, you are a bit apprehensive because you sense a stiff challenge ahead, you are right. With all of its rewards, matrimony makes demands. Like life itself, it requires that we possess the desire and the will to grow as people. Those, therefore, who may be looking, first and foremost, for what they can get out of it are in for a big disappointment because conjugal love means giving rather than getting. It means having to say one is sorry and saying it often. Instead of using your spouse for your own ends, you will find yourself sacrificing for the good of the marriage. Time and time again, you and your partner will extend yourselves to the absolute limit because love that is true knows no bounds, and true love is the only kind that lasts.

A great saint by the name of Catherine of Siena once had a vision that God was offering her many crosses, some small, others

---

[1] Pope John Paul II, in his *Letter to Families* (1994), calls marriage "a true vocation" as well as "a great mystery" (quoting Saint Paul). See nos. 18-19.

large. Anxious to please she selected the heaviest. "No," said the Lord, "that one is not for you. It is reserved for married couples." Catherine's insight may be a trifle tart, but it serves as a useful corrective to the prevailing notion that it is somehow easier to be married than to lead a chaste single life. Where is the evidence for such an assumption? Whatever our state in life, whether we are single, married, or bound by religious vows, there will be trials. The thing to bear in mind is that God has promised each and every one of us all the means necessary to carry on, and to carry on beautifully, provided we do what we can to cooperate. And that, of course, is where pre-Cana comes in. Before athletes enter competition, they prepare. Before soldiers go into battle, they train. And the same holds true of marriage. As in sport and combat, there is no substitute for preparation. Marriage handbooks may not simulate actual "field" conditions, but in many ways they can come close, and it will be the aim of the following pages to come as close as possible.

Even if there were no trend afoot to treat matrimony lightly and to discount the whole idea of lifelong fidelity, there would still be a need to prepare for marriage, just as one prepares for any significant event in life. Priestly vocations are brought to fruition by years of seminary training. Ambitious parents aiming at a prestigious Ivy League education for their youngster go out of their way to enroll the child in the right nursery school. A lengthy apprenticeship is necessary to become a full-fledged plumber or electrician. Many newlyweds anticipate parenthood by attending a series of childbirth courses. Yet ironically, in one of the most vital commitments of all, marriage itself, the only courses seem to appear after the fact: "Parenting Without a Partner," "Handling Your Divorce," or "Making It in the Post-Marriage Singles World."

Curiously enough, the Catholic Church is one of the few institutions in the world that requires some type of formal instruction before marriage, and this is due, in large part, to her insistence on the sacramental and binding nature of the union.

As Catholics, we reject categorically the idea of divorce and remarriage, believing that no marriage, however ill-advised or troubled, is ever beyond redemption. When we pledge our loyalty "for better or worse," "in sickness and in health," we are saying in effect that nothing, absolutely nothing, can ever invalidate our commitment: not cancer, not paralysis, not childlessness, not alcoholism, not even infidelity. Separation may be warranted in extreme cases, but never divorce and remarriage. This is one of the cardinal tenets of Catholic teaching, firmly in place for nearly two thousand years, and it comes directly from Christ, as well as Saint Paul.[2] Jesus restored marriage to its original ideal after it had been debased by polygamy, divorce, and adultery.

We are all aware that ecclesiastical authorities have been known, on occasion, to grant a declaration of nullity (commonly known as an "annulment"), stating that, in the absence of certain preconditions, a marriage never took place (in the sense that the contract between consenting parties that is required for marriage was never valid to begin with).[3] Critics are quick to suggest that annulment is merely divorce, Catholic style. But this is not so. There may have been abuses, particularly in the United States in recent years, owing to the human side of the Church, and such abuses may have undermined the Church's credibility.[4] But we should not be put off. Clerical compromisers are a well-known breed in Church history, leaders who capitulated to the "powers that be" either out of weakness or genuine pastoral concern. What is heartening is that the Church is still the Church. She is still teaching essentially what she taught two millennia ago. Christ's vicar on earth has been totally consistent over the years in holding that once a valid union is contracted, it is indissoluble—that is, unbreakable. Prominent figures such as Bishop John Fisher and Sir Thomas More of England gave their very lives in defense of

---

[2] See Appendix B.
[3] See Appendix C.
[4] See Appendix L.

this principle, which remains to this day one of the most precious jewels in the crown of our faith.

Apart from the fact that divorce has been linked with the likelihood of early death from strokes, hypertension, respiratory and intestinal cancer; apart, too, from the fact that children from broken homes are more likely to do poorly in school, abuse drugs, break the law, and attempt suicide, nothing could be more positive or more healthy than the Catholic stand on indissolubility.[5] And the reason is simple. Only if one is committed to giving one's all, only when one is shielded from the temptation to look for a way out when caught in the eye of the storm, does marriage come into its own. Conversely, the moment one accepts the possibility of divorce and remarriage, even for serious reasons, then one is sanctioning divorce on demand—for whose reasons are not serious? And with what result? All marriages, even sound ones, wind up on shaky ground. Given today's moral climate, with its stress on situation ethics, married couples are an endangered species. The fact that half of them choose to separate is a pretty sure sign that many, if not most, of the others must be struggling just to keep up appearances. One might add, on the basis of statistics, that the rate of failure for those who remarry is staggeringly high, higher even than the rate associated with first marriages. Furthermore, according to a recent survey conducted by researchers at the University of Virginia, seventy-two percent of all divorcées are convinced, within two years of marital breakup, that their divorce was a mistake.[6]

Naturally, the more serious we are about marriage, the more anxious we will be to prepare, especially if we believe there can be no turning back. It is an interesting commentary on today's society

---

[5] Philip Yancey, "God is Good for You," *Catholic Digest* (February 1992), 2. Judges have required applicants for divorce to take upward of four hours of courses to familiarize themselves with the many ills visited on the children of divorced parents, *The New York Times* (January 23, 1992), C8.

[6] *National Catholic Register* (May 24, 1992), 5 (the proportion for men was also high: sixty-one percent).

that jurors selected in some places for federal trial duty are likely to receive a more thorough cross-examination than many young people contemplating marriage. The judge will try to ascertain if they have any emotional blocks, prejudices, or compromising relationships, any "chips on the shoulder," so to speak, that could prove damaging. They will be quizzed on their understanding of the essentials of the law and asked if, once in deliberation, they expect to have enough gumption to stick to their opinion even if they find themselves a minority of one. Attorneys on both sides will also want to know if potential jurors are humble enough to reassess their position should they be convinced by fellow jurors, in the heat of argument, that they are wrong. Humility . . . courage . . . understanding . . . emotional fitness—these are the very same traits required for a successful marriage.

No couple wants to have their relationship examined with a fine-tooth comb and to have questions tossed at them once they have settled on a definite course of action. But those who submit cheerfully can rest assured that if their intentions are pleasing in God's sight, nothing on the face of the earth is going to thwart them. If, on the one hand, there are underlying problems, now is the time to face them. If you are headed for trouble, now is the time to reconsider. If, on the other hand, you are on the right track, your chance for a smooth and happy adjustment will be greatly enhanced by going into marriage with both eyes open. Love need not be blind. The fewer surprises the better.

≈ Chapter 2 ≈
Preparation

Asking the Right Questions

Presumably, by the time you are engaged, you have dated a number of different individuals. Not that this is essential, but ask yourself if you would want to buy the first house shown to you by a real estate broker. It is much the same in the choice of a husband or wife. A good way to become aware of differences is to get to know people from varied backgrounds. Obviously, the more you have in common with your spouse in the way of goals and ideals, hobbies and interests, the better the prospect for lasting happiness.

It goes without saying, too, that you chose each other for the right reasons and have enjoyed one another's company for a reasonable period of time prior to engagement. Hopefully, by the time you became serious, you were able to observe how your partner handles stress in various forms. How do you relate to one another's friends and relatives? How do you react to disappointments and setbacks? Infatuation based on the glamour of a few dates or on sheer physical attraction is bound to fade and, if you are sensible, you are not marrying simply to please your parents or to gain financial security. Neither are you undertaking a lifelong commitment merely to raise your social status or to satisfy some biological urge. Such motives will not suffice to carry you through life.

Let us assume, in addition, that you have considered a religious vocation, along with a chaste single life, as alternatives to marriage, for only if you have decided, after prayerful reflection, that marriage is the way God is calling you and your fiancée to carry out your mission in life (which is to know Him, to love Him, and to serve Him) should you proceed with your wedding plans.

To go a step further, how do you feel about the possibility of having children? If you are not willing to accept them as a gift from God or are presently unable to support them financially, it would be wise to postpone your wedding until such time as things change.

How noble it is to share with God in the conception of immortal life and to lead young souls along the road to sanctity! Procreation may not be the only end of marriage. But it is the primary end, central to the plan of creation. One might almost call it a "mission" since each child is not only a gift bestowed on the family *by* God, but also a great gift of the family *to* God. In addition, children contribute immeasurably to the growth of such traits as sensitivity, patience, wisdom, endurance, and holiness in their parents.

Marriage as a vocation aims at nothing less than the rearing of saints who will provide the "leaven" that our world so desperately needs and who will ultimately take their place beside their Maker in heaven. Granted, parents cannot guarantee the salvation of their children. But neither is this required of them. All God asks is that they do their part. The rest is up to Him, in conjunction with the children themselves, and we can rest assured that He will hold up His end of the bargain. Francis Thompson's "Hound of Heaven" never rests! So there is every reason to rejoice and be glad.

As for couples who are not blessed with offspring, we can be sure that they are richly compensated in other ways. God is all loving and all good. More on this later.

And what if you are planning to marry a non-Catholic? The closer your partner comes to sharing your moral and religious values, the happier and more stable your union is going to be, as religion is bound to affect the way a person thinks and behaves. In spite of the optimism of those who assume that conjugal affection will bridge all gaps, religious differences constitute a definite basis for conflict, especially in regard to having children and providing for their education. To their credit, both parties may be strong and morally upright. Both may hope to win over the other in the long run. Ironically, the finer and more zealous the parties to such a match, the greater the likelihood of tension. Non-Catholics have as much of a right to want their children molded along cherished lines of thought and belief as Catholics. This is an area, therefore, that needs to be well thought out and thoroughly discussed before marriage so that resolutions can be made as to how and when the family will pray together as a unit and how the children will be encouraged (not merely *permitted*, but *encouraged*) to grow in the practice of their faith.

For many years, the Church forbade Catholics to marry persons of another religion, and exceptions were made only for grave reasons. Why? Because experience indicates that "mixed" marriages (and this includes marriage to a lukewarm Catholic, as well as to a non-Catholic) are generally a source of discord and unhappiness for the entire family. All too often, such marriages result in religious indifference or loss of faith on the part of the Catholic, as well as a home atmosphere detrimental to the religious formation of the children. Both parties should be aware of the risks so they are prepared to make up the difference in other ways. In particular, there must be a clear understanding that one's offspring are to be raised and educated in the faith. This is Church law and, as such, it binds the conscience of the Catholic.

Finally, how do you feel about engagement itself? You should be elated. Anxiety about plans and arrangements is natural. There may even be some inner doubt about one's ability to "measure up," but you should be happy and relieved to be on your way.

Beyond this, engagement calls for a certain degree of vigilance and self-control. Now is the time to display the kind of fidelity that will be indispensable later on. Obviously, there should be no flirting with third parties or playing hard to get. Neither should one be taking physical liberties of the kind reserved for marriage.[1]

---

[1] According to the Catechism, engaged couples "should reserve for marriage the expressions of affection that belong to married love" (no. 2350).

Even if prolonged kissing, petting, hugging, and necking of the type calculated to arouse sexual passion were not sinful, all of this would be risky because of where it is likely to lead. The marriage contract, to be valid, requires freedom of choice, and such freedom is necessarily impaired by excessive sexual involvement. The moment one becomes involved on the physical level to the point where marriage becomes something that is "owed," rather than freely given, one forfeits an important element of choice. There must be no high-pressure salesman standing over you when you make the most critical decision of your life. Many an argument for divorce turns on the premise that a person did not really "will" marriage, but rather slipped into it or was pressured by force of circumstance.

So, in a word, if you are trying to guard your courtship and take the high road, keep it up. This is the prudent, as well as the correct, course if you are serious about the future.

It is easy to fall for the line that premarital sex, in the sense of "living together," helps couples find out whether or not they are compatible. Nothing could be farther from the truth. Sex outside of marriage cannot come anywhere near simulating the conditions of marital union because the situations are radically different, with different responsibilities, different expectations, different commitments, and an entirely different psychological "feel." One's mate outside marriage is apt to appear more attractive (or less so) than he or she would actually be wearing a wedding band. Just as apples and oranges are similar in shape but not in taste, so too, with licit and illicit sex. Sin is never a good place to discover the truth. Besides, it is rare that two people who love one another for the right reasons and who are compatible in other ways turn out to have serious difficulties expressing affection on the physical plane.

By one recent estimate, forty percent of those who live together before marriage never make it to the altar, and of those who do, the divorce rate is significantly higher than it is for other couples. Fornicators are thus putting whatever children may be born of such a union at grave risk.[2] In other words, apart from the sanction upheld by every major religion, common sense alone would dictate the avoidance of an act which, in the view of psychologists, is likely to leave permanent scars. Once you have given yourself totally to another human being, it is doubtful that you will ever be able to do so again in quite the same way.

And what if you are already on the wrong road? It is never too late to turn back. With a sincere desire for God's forgiveness and a firm purpose of amendment, you can still receive the Sacrament of Matrimony worthily. Although fornication (the name given by the Bible to premarital sex) is a definite offense against God, as well as against the virtue and honor of one's betrothed, the Lord is unfailingly kind and compassionate. It is just that He expects three very definite things of us: contrition, confession, and penance. In a word, if you have engaged in premarital intercourse or if you are living with your intended spouse, now is the time to stop, go to Confession, and do whatever penance is prescribed by the priest. In this way, you will retain your freedom, and God will smile on you in the way the father of the Gospel story smiled on his prodigal son. Let the white of the bridal gown be a true symbol of virtue, the diamond a real token of lasting happiness. Be honest with yourselves, with society, and with your Maker.

No one would claim that chastity is an easy virtue to live. If it were, everyone would be living it. No, it can be difficult, which is why long engagements are not usually recommended. Nevertheless, it is well within the range of the possible for those who are (a) convinced that this is what the Lord is asking of them, and (b) confident that, if they persist in prayer, their Heavenly Father will furnish them with grace sufficient to avoid places and situations that are likely to be occasions of sin. Jesus Himself said, "Ask, and it will be given you; seek, and you will find; knock, and it will be opened to you" (Mt. 7:7).

---

[2] *Our Sunday Visitor* (December 27, 1992), 23. See also *The New York Times* (June 9, 1989), A1; *National Catholic Register* (May 7, 1989), 5.

Such counsel may sound almost quaint at a time when we are bombarded on every side by advice of a different kind. But with the Lord's help, all things are possible, and if, for some reason, the kind of restraint to which we are referring seems out of reach, you have reason to be concerned, for if there is anything the married state demands it is self-possession. Without this, one is only leading oneself and one's spouse-to-be down the primrose path.

Ours is an age in which the statistics on abortion, venereal disease, teenage suicide, and divorce are sky-high.[3] At the same time, this very society which has proven such a failure when it comes to sexual adjustment, continues to palm off its trendy wisdom on millions of young people who crave a "modern" lifestyle.

Think about it. If there were a village somewhere in the world with a life expectancy of twenty-three and where four out of six infants died before reaching the age of five, would you want to adopt its diet and imitate its customs? If you believe it makes any sense in a culture such as ours to attempt to be "one of the crowd," then a Catholic marriage is not for you. If, on the other hand, you are open to a code of sexual conduct with a proven track record, one that is perfectly capable of serving the present age, then proceed. We cannot say that "everyone is doing it." But then you are not "everyone." Hopefully, you will have second thoughts before setting yourself up for a life of disillusionment which seems to be more and more the common lot.

Engagement

Engagement is a time to draw closer to God, the source of all happiness, and if you are sensible, you will make this approach a joint venture. Why not arrange to receive the sacraments as a

---

[3] There is no nation in the world, not even Sweden, where the divorce rate is as high as it is in the United States. *Christian Science Monitor* (January 26, 1987), 21. According to *Our Sunday Visitor* (December 27, 1992), 23, "Divorce tripled since 1960, and illegitimacy soared fourfold, even though abortions tripled over the past 20 years."

couple so as to pave the way for the kind of pattern you hope to establish later on? Perhaps, too, one or both of you will write a wedding prayer that can be recited down through the crowded years of your marriage, one that will evoke fond memories of a glorious day. Why not attend an extra weekday Mass? The Holy Eucharist is powerful. If you are fortunate enough to live or work in an area where celebration of the Liturgy is frequent, you may find that you can receive Communion before work, during lunch break, or on the way home. Accompany your preparation for marriage with sincere daily prayer for a partner whom you can freely and truly love; one you truly wish "to have and to hold, from this day forward, for better, for worse, for richer, for poorer, in sickness and in health, until death do us part." Could you squeeze in a Rosary while you ride a bus or wait in line, or perhaps sign up for a weekend retreat?

Granted, engagement is also a time to make wedding plans, to take stock of finances, and to think seriously about what will be needed to maintain a household. Generally speaking, you would be ill-advised to start out under someone else's roof, well-intentioned as that someone else might be. Nor would it be advisable to enter marriage under a heavy load of financial obligation. A fair number of divorce cases involve people who are head-over-heels in debt. When one of my wife's college friends suddenly decided to postpone her marriage originally scheduled immediately after graduation, everyone was shocked, wondering if the courtship had soured. They were even more astounded when she announced that because she and her fiancé could not afford children, they were not tying the knot until they could; hence the postponement. As far as we know, this couple is still happily married.

When I was growing up, breadwinners could usually count on earning a "living wage," enabling one or the other parent, normally the wife, to stay home with the children. Since this is no longer the rule and since such expedients as artificial birth control, sterilization, and abortion are morally impermissible, couples are wise to build some kind of a financial base before becoming engaged. In some cases, this could mean living with one's parents for an interval while holding down a full-time job, winning promotion, and saving every penny. In others, it might be a matter of living alone and saving less, but delaying engagement or marriage still further until the basic elements of financial security are in place. If, in addition, there is a mutual willingness to sacrifice once the marriage takes place by living simply, this could well mean the difference between children who benefit from "hands-on" parental supervision and those who do not.

Finally, engagement is a time to take one last look at oneself and one's spouse-to-be to make doubly sure there are no impediments to the marriage.[4] Ask yourself if you respect one another as persons. Are there any obvious character flaws in the picture such as selfishness, pride, or intemperance which could interfere with what God intended to be a happy way of life? Strive to draw your partner out on all sensitive issues, so that if there are differences of opinion, they will not be left to come as a surprise, perhaps even a shock, after the formal exchange of vows. At the very end of this book, you will find thirty-one thought-provoking questions geared to a deeper understanding of what real communication between the parties to an engagement is all about. I encourage you to read them over carefully and then discuss them individually with your husband- or wife-to-be.

If, at any point along the way, you sense something to be seriously wrong, you are morally free, indeed *morally obligated*, to terminate your relationship. A certain amount of trepidation is normal on the eve of such a momentous event. But even if, five minutes before you walk down the aisle, you have second thoughts, it is better to be safe than sorry, despite all the disappointment and embarrassment this may entail. Ten broken engagements are better than a single broken marriage. Parents,

---

[4] See Appendix C.

for their part, have a responsibility to make this clear to their children, regardless of how many plans they may have made or how much they may have spent.

Your Wedding

There are many ways of preparing for the big day. While going over your wedding ceremony with the priest, you will ordinarily want to request a nuptial Mass so you can receive Communion in the company of any wedding guests who may be eligible. The only exception would be in the case of a mixed marriage, where one might wish to avoid a display of disunity on the first day of marriage. There is usually a selection of prayers for the wedding ceremony, as well as a variety of readings, and you are entitled to your choice. Then, too, in addition to familiarizing yourself with the ceremony itself, you will want to spend some time preparing for your role as host or hostess. Appropriately enough, bride and groom are called upon in the first formal act of their marriage to reach out to others. Some guests may have come from far away at considerable expense, and a gracious way of thanking them for their presence and support is to spend a moment or two with each of them and to have a few thoughtful words on tap. Try, if you can, to bone up in advance on guests you may not know personally.

Your First Night Together

With all that it takes to carry off a wedding reception, bride and groom may be exhausted by the end of the day, especially the bride, who generally bears the burden of preparation. Your first night is not, for this reason, a good time to apply pressure of any kind or to feel any sense of compulsion. The more sensitive the groom in this regard, the more he will merit the esteem and confidence of his bride. The greater also will be the chance for a happy honeymoon.

Honeymooning

Not every couple can afford an exotic trip abroad, nor is this necessary. Consider yourself blessed if you can get away to a place that affords some privacy, even if only for a few days, in order to relax and savor the exhilaration of new beginnings. We have all heard about harrowing honeymoons, but this happens only to those who aim to achieve too much too quickly. If you concentrate exclusively on making the other person happy in the most affectionate way you know how, neither of you will be disappointed, for it is only when one expects the lights to start flashing and the most intimate parts of a relationship to function perfectly from the very first moment that there is likely to be difficulty.

The physiological side of marriage is like a flower that takes time for all of its radiant petals to unfold. Certain forms of satisfaction may elude you for months, even years. Worry not. The marriage act is only one mode of expression among many and not necessarily the most important. Those who are truly in love will bear with delays and setbacks, confident that, in the long run, the solicitude they demonstrate for the feelings of their partner will yield fruit a hundredfold. Authentic love seeks intimacy in countless ways, and when this is the case, the sexual element has a way of falling into line. Finally, whatever you do in the course of trial and error, never lose your sense of humor. There is a side to the art of becoming one flesh that can only be described as comical, and you will find that a hearty laugh, now and then, can do wonders to put things in proper perspective.

Settling Down

The experts tell us that a partnership normally passes through three stages: (1) romance, (2) disillusionment, and (3) either a breakthrough to true love (which comes with patience and perseverance) or loneliness, distance, and pain. It is the third phase that is critical; but because its outcome depends on how the other two are understood, a look at disillusionment is in order.

Some kind of letdown following the honeymoon is almost certain to occur. Most husbands and wives find themselves hard pressed merely to cope with the strain of daily living. There may also be a gap between what is expected of marriage and what marriage as an institution is capable of delivering. Although people faced with a deteriorating relationship often believe that the fault lies with their spouse, the fact is that no human being, however angelic, is equipped to guarantee the happiness of another. This is something only God Himself can do, and even He does not promise instant results. There will be periods of estrangement in even the happiest home when one or the other party is likely to feel misunderstood and dejected. There will also be intervals when a perfectly good husband or wife will drive everyone up the wall. Be patient. Wait for the sun to come out from behind those clouds. It will.

Still another reason for disillusionment is that the bride and groom may discover that they have little in common. Assume, for the sake of argument, that boy meets girl on a ski trip, and they decide to get married on the basis of some fun they had on the slopes. Once they are married, there may not be any more ski trips, at least not for a while. So they settle down and find conversation awkward, decisions difficult. Suppose, in another instance, that a disproportionate amount of the couple's attention before marriage centered on ways and means of obtaining parental approval or, alternately, on the number of wedding guests to be invited and canapés to be served. After all is in place, these same people who occupied themselves with romantic plans and strategies may find themselves with few, if any, shared interests, much less common goals on which to build.

A fourth factor which helps to explain post-honeymoon blues is the effect that relaxation tends to have on human behavior. Where once we tried to look our best, we now feel free to "let our hair down." As dates, we may have been sensitive, courteous, and attentive. Now, all of a sudden, we feel we can take each other for granted. Faults, once hidden, begin to surface under the strain of budgeting. There is a need to adjust sexually, to adapt to in-laws, and to hold down a job that overnight becomes vital to the security of two people, instead of just one. Similarly, a couple will often find that, hard as they may try, they have less uninterrupted time together once they are married, and their income may not allow for the kind of diversion or the type of wardrobe to which they were accustomed. Suddenly, they have to make decisions that are potentially divisive, and if they are not careful, they begin to lose touch. Fears, hopes, and desires go unexpressed, frustration mounts, and communication breaks down.

If you should find yourself in this situation, just remember that marriage was designed by Almighty God to last forever, and *it will* if you take your vows in good faith and with determination to go the distance. One of the answers to marital letdown in the early stages is to recognize it for what it is and to know that family harmony takes time, as well as effort.

Are there cases of chronically troubled partnerships that will resist even the most heroic efforts at healing? Yes. There may be times when marriage becomes a cross that one must carry all the way to the grave. You can be certain, however, that if this is so, it will be your ticket to heaven. I like to think that Jesus is going to say to worn-out spouses who have persevered to the end what He said to the good thief on Calvary: "today you will be with me in Paradise" (Lk. 23:43). In any event, the answer is not to shop around for a new partner. Far better an imperfect union, even a separation, than the most perfect divorce. And this goes for the children, as well as the parents—especially the children. Studies indicate that the younger victims of divorce and remarriage suffer the most.

But let us not dwell on the negative. Doubtless, your match will be all you ever hoped for and more. You will seek out solutions to problems as they arise; joy will outweigh sadness; faith will overcome all obstacles. This is the ideal, and there is no reason to believe that it is not a realizable ideal for those who are willing to work at it.

The Ten Commandments of Communication

Let me explain what I mean by "willing to work at it."

Who is not familiar with the soap opera stereotype of an unhappy marriage? John hides behind his newspaper when he is not glued to the tube or out drinking with the boys, while his wife Joan runs a chaotic household and spends her time on the phone with girlfriends or relatives. At the dinner table, neither party has much to say. John takes little interest in Joan's problems. She could care less about the things that occupy him at work. When they do converse over a family meal, it is more by way of criticism than positive reinforcement. So the conversation sputters along in dribs and drabs, directed mainly at the children.

According to marriage counselors, communication breakdowns such as this are not only ominous, they are also very common, affecting a broad cross-section of society. And while they may reflect a variety of marital problems, they are often the cause of such problems. At the same time—and here is the rub—they are eminently avoidable. Communication is an art and, as such, it can be cultivated. The husband and wife who communicate with ease have an automatic handle on almost any problem that may arise. At the very least, they are able to grapple with ongoing challenges as a couple. There is, moreover, no reason why one can't learn the skill of communication just as one would learn any other skill.

Here, then, for those willing to work at it, are some elementary rules of thumb:

RULE 1: *Make time for each other*, particularly after the arrival of children. Be single-minded about setting aside a certain period each day when you can relax with your partner and unwind. It could be half an hour in the morning before the kids are up; it could be an hour in the evening after they are asleep. But it should be time you can count on because communication, to be effective, requires effort. There is much to be said for planning some sort of weekly "date." Stealing away for a meal, even if only to your local diner, taking a leisurely stroll, or going for a relaxing drive will help to keep the dating spirit alive. If you have youngsters at home and are without a sitter, you might bring in some deli sandwiches so you can enjoy a video or TV program after the rest of the family is safely tucked away. Whatever you do, try to make the few moments you spend together as memorable and pleasant as possible.

You might also give some thought to the cultivation of leisure time activities that bring you together. I used to love the game of bridge, and although my wife, Sylvia, knew nothing about it, she was happy to take lessons. Eventually, though, she decided that bridge was not the game for her, and so we found another pastime that could be shared. By the same token, both of us used to enjoy a brisk game of tennis with partners of our own speed. Today, however, we would rather spend the little time we have rallying with one another and chasing balls for the sheer fun and fellow-ship of it. A couple might decide to take up an entirely new sport like bowling, again with an eye to keeping the family together. *Being* together and *staying* together are two sides of the same coin.

RULE 2: *Take nothing for granted.* Marital relations rarely stand still. If they don't thrive, they languish. It is important, therefore, to ask questions while keeping a hot line open to your partner at all times. In business, the boss is always checking to make sure the secretary understands what needs to be done; the attitude is one of "give me a buzz if there's a problem." So too, lifelong collaborators should be saying the same thing at every juncture, anxious to know how they are doing. There may be virtue in the "strong, silent type," but such virtue lies more in the strength than in the silence. If one party is reticent by nature, the other should not give up. The ideal couple will converse about all aspects of life, including matters of delicacy, for unless both parties can deal verbally with issues across the board, it will be hard for either of them to meet the full range of the other's needs and expectations. One might add that children, too, should have their forum. Oftentimes, parental willingness to hold a family conference for the airing of proper concerns will do wonders to restore peace and harmony.

RULE 3: *Learn to listen* so that others will want to confide in you. Don't get angry or upset at what you hear. Never say, "I told you so." And don't interrupt.

RULE 4: *Be patient and discreet in drawing the other person out.* Some spouses may want to be left alone for a spell before they open up. There may be times, too, when your partner will be talked out. At moments like this, you might decide to take a quiet walk together simply to show that you care. Whatever you do, never "dump" on a mate the moment he or she arrives home from work. Allow time for the new arrival to wash up, have a snack, and look over the mail. Later on there will be enough time to catch up on the latest in your respective spheres.

RULE 5: *Accept criticism gracefully and learn to apologize.* Learning to take criticism is good, but better still is asking for it on occasion and being quick to apologize. The phrase "I'm sorry" is a wonderful all-purpose solvent capable of cutting through the gummiest mounds of double-talk and misunderstanding.

RULE 6: *Avoid nagging.* Instead of asking directly for certain favors when your wife or husband is distracted, you might consider writing a little "love note" that can be left on a desk or bureau for action when convenient. If you need something badly enough and one or two gentle reminders do not suffice, it may be time to sit down and calmly explain the urgency of the problem from your point of view. Occasionally, though, even this will not work, and you may simply have to accept what you cannot change, offering it up as a share in the Lord's suffering.

RULE 7: *Express gratitude* for little things, as well as big ones. There is a tendency in each of us to do exactly the opposite. Just as our better half emerges from the kitchen with a freshly baked pie, we are apt to blurt out a preference for chocolate cake. However inadvertent such remarks may be, they can put a real strain on the marriage because next in importance to the phrase "I love you" (which cannot be heard too often) comes "thank you." Chances are that if we give thanks or praise ten times for every request or criticism, the ratio will be about right. Did he do a good job on the driving? Then acknowledge it. Did she put together a specially lovely floral arrangement? Then notice it.

RULE 8: *Learn the ground rules for fighting.* Squabbles are a part of every marriage and they are apt to occur over relatively minor things. Still, they should be kept within bounds and avoided whenever possible. Although a clearing of the air may be healthy, loud disagreements can be destructive, as well as exhausting, and they also tend to demoralize the children.

While one should try to keep the lines of communication open, there is no need to confront all prickly issues every time they arise. There is such a thing as agreeing to disagree. Sometimes, it is the better part of valor, when you sense a storm brewing, to retreat, and if lightning strikes, not to strike back. Bruising your mate by calling names, shouting, or leveling charges is almost certain to be counterproductive.

Should you sense, at any time, that you may have hurt your partner's feelings, intentionally or unintentionally, be quick to make up. Saint Paul tells us never to let the sun go down on our anger (Eph. 4:26). Never go to bed angry or hurt without tendering at least one kiss as a peace offering, along with a sincere apology. We may see ourselves as the injured party. But we can always say, "I'm sorry, honey, if I've hurt your feelings; I didn't mean to." Such magnanimity, coupled with a willingness to postpone discussion, will eliminate much bitterness. Be prompt to say you're sorry, and if you are beaten to the punch, respond graciously. Jesus was once asked how often one should forgive. "As many as seven times?" queried Peter. "I do not say to you seven times," said Our Lord, "but seventy times seven!" (cf. Mt. 18:21-22). Beyond this, once we have forgiven, we must do our best to forget. To pout or withhold affection after a verbal skirmish is to poison the domestic atmosphere. Did you ever hear the story about the two men who liked to discuss their home life? One of them remarked that he loved his wife, but every time they got into an argument, she became "historical." "You mean hysterical," said the other. "No, historical," insisted the first. "She keeps bringing up the past."

RULE 9: *Keep confidences confidential.* The best way to shut down the all-important communication process is to reveal family secrets. Some of us may feel that we are only confiding in "best friends." But once we are married, we have only one "best friend," our partner. Do not complain, especially to relatives. Bear in mind, too, that the right kind of friend will strengthen your marriage by causing you to feel satisfied, rather than dissatisfied.

RULE 10: *Use sex for the purpose intended by God.* At its best, marital intercourse can be an extraordinarily beautiful way of saying, "I love you." At its worst, it is likely to convey just the opposite meaning. One hears much these days about "having sex." What a contradiction in terms! If the procreative act is anything, it is a supreme act of *giving*; and, because it transmits the tenderest of messages in the tenderest of ways, it can be one of the most effective forms of communication. One's message will be distorted, however, if not altogether lost, if it involves manipulation or if too much emphasis is placed on the physical.

In Sum

Chances are that if you give yourself unreservedly with one eye trained on the hereafter, your marriage will not only survive but prosper. Storms there will be, along with periods of aridity. You may be faced with a rash of catastrophes when God seems to be looking the other way. But there is no reason to panic. If you can't resolve an issue, see a mutual friend or counselor who is sound in the faith. Above all, remember that love is not a feeling that comes and goes depending upon one's mood. It is a lifelong commitment which, like fine wine, improves with age. Someone once remarked that "love is what you've been through together," and how true. Perseverance is nine-tenths of the battle and, given such an attitude, communication crises, if and when they occur, will only bring you closer together. In the end, you will be more secure as a couple, and better off as a team, for having braved the winds of adversity.

⤜ Chapter 3 ⤛
Family Life

Just as every person is unique, so it is with families. The home you make for yourselves and for your children will differ in unexpected ways from the one in which you grew up. While it is only natural to want to duplicate one's childhood environment down to the last detail, it is also unrealistic. A man may have had a mother who fastidiously turned back his sheets every night and folded his bedspread. Now that he is married, he finds that his wife's strengths lie elsewhere. In the same way, the wife's father may have been diligent about keeping his car clean and fixing things around the house, while the man she marries will let the car go for weeks without a wash, contractors must be called in for minor repairs, and bills begin to mount. Her husband has talents of his own, but she can't help missing that paternal touch. When she asks him to take out the garbage, he does it grudgingly. Mom never put Dad to work this way. And when he requests his evening meal at 6:00 p.m., the hour to which he is accustomed, she takes offense; her family never sat down to dinner before 7:30. On top of this, she is a night owl who retires at 2:00 a.m. and likes to sleep late, while he collapses at 10:00 p.m., only to be up, bright-eyed and bushy-tailed, at 5:00 a.m.

A thousand and one similar situations, all equally petty, are likely to present themselves in the early months of marriage, and the future of the partnership may well depend on how smoothly one makes the necessary adjustments.

Learning to Adapt

Since marriage brings together people from separate and distinct backgrounds, there will be differences on almost every conceivable level. The more alike a couple is in overall values, the less the likelihood of friction. But even in the most ideal match, one partner or the other is going to be more practical in this way or that, more refined, more gregarious. One or the other will be more athletic or more artistic. Such differences can be refreshing because "opposites attract." Nevertheless, along with such discrepancy comes a need to hone the skill of conciliation which, in turn, requires communication.

Let us assume, for instance, that after love-making, a husband's mood shifts, and his wife, who is slower to disengage, feels abandoned. Hopefully, she will confide in him, and he will meet her more than halfway when he senses that her feelings in this regard are more intense than his own. Perhaps, in another type of situation, the wife, who was schooled by her family to conduct lengthy postmortems after every social event, is married to a man who feels ill at ease raking company over the coals the moment the party is over. He reveals his sensitivity to her when she is in a receptive mood, and if she finds that her feelings run less deeply than his, she acts accordingly. In a similar scenario, the husband may be the type who was taught to verbalize disagreements and talk everything out on the spot. His wife, on the other hand, is accustomed to letting a good deal go and to warding off confrontation. In this instance, Mr. "Settle-it-right-away" will demonstrate a willingness to defer the moment of truth, while Mrs. "Talk-about-it-later" will address more issues head-on.

Some of this may sound picayune, but it is the stuff of which separations and divorces are made. Unless there is some great moral principle at stake, don't hesitate to be the one who does the yielding.

And what if both parties prove adamant? Toss a coin or work out a formula. In the case of the night owl and early bird, she might go to bed a couple of hours earlier than usual while he might retire a couple of hours later, and if she doesn't fall right off to sleep, she will read a book while he accustoms himself to sleeping with the light on. Or take something as simple as the evening meal. Suppose he is always watching TV or tinkering with the car when she calls him to dinner—by the time he reaches the table, the main course is cold. This is something an experienced couple will try to resolve at an opportune time. Possibly, as part of the bargain, she will agree to serve her summons earlier with a "Honey, dinner will be ready in five minutes," while he, for his part, will make more of an effort to pry himself loose. Different couples facing different problems will hit upon different solutions. The main thing is for each couple to be imaginative in coping with the challenges that are sure to come their way.

Traditional and Non-Traditional Roles

In today's world, where women are often employed full-time outside the home, some equitable way must be found to share domestic duties. It may be that if one party balances the checkbook, empties wastebaskets, and cleans the bathroom, the other will vacuum and dust. Any division of labor will do so long as it is fair and efficient.

Husbands and wives are capable of doing a great many things traditionally reserved for the opposite sex, and doing them well. However, there is always the danger, in an age of accelerated social change and experimentation, that one will go overboard. So don't hesitate to backtrack should you find yourself departing from the norm established by your parents. She may say she doesn't mind going to a gas station with the car; he may insist that he doesn't mind cooking; both may be sincere. Yet within a short while, both may yearn inwardly for a more conventional lifestyle. Tradition did not become tradition by accident!

The Spirit of Partnership

Marriage thrives on husbandly, as well as wifely, deference. Although Scripture makes it clear that wives should be submissive to their husbands, relying on them for leadership in the broadest sense of the word, it also says that husbands should love their wives as they love their own bodies and as Christ loves His Church. For the man, such love implies tender solicitude and steady support, along with frequent consultation. The wife, who is his equal in dignity before God, deserves a voice in all family decisions, especially those that affect her directly. But beyond the question of rights, her input on a wide range of issues will be useful. Two heads are commonly better than one, and she is bound to be more knowledgeable in certain areas than her husband.

True, he is head of the household and, like a corporation's chairman of the board, is responsible for the smooth running and overall well-being of the family. But this does not mean that he has to take personal charge of all areas, especially when his wife may be better qualified. It also assumes that he is in possession of his faculties and capable of demonstrating conjugal love of the type described by Saint Paul. In the case of absentee husbands and fathers, the woman may find herself forced by default to step into the breach. But this is neither the norm nor the ideal. The good wife will encourage her husband even if he is less than perfect, just as she will consult regularly and give careful thought to his opinion.

Husbandly solicitude could mean attending to the children while she goes to a meeting. It might call for doing the dishes when he would rather be watching a ball game on TV. Whatever the case, if each partner tries to make things easier and more pleasant for the other, volunteering on occasion to tackle unpleasant chores, even to the point of friendly argument—call it a "heavenly argument"—if each strives to give the other the better portion in life, there will be little danger of marital breakdown.

Husbandly "headship" is a notion that is touched upon by

both Peter and Paul, the latter at least three separate times, suggesting that it may have been as hot an issue in those days as it is today.[1] Obviously, women have entered many fields formerly reserved for men, and some have assumed the role of breadwinner. This, however, does not alter the dynamics of conjugal interaction. Suppose, in a comparable situation, that the father of a particular family were to fall ill. His teenage son might have to drop out of school and find employment to help support his parents. But regardless of what the son did or didn't do, he would still be the son and, as such, obliged to show filial respect.

Keeping the Dating Spirit Alive

Marriage, like courtship, flourishes in an atmosphere of small, voluntary acts of kindness. A rose wrapped in baby's breath that one brings home unexpectedly with a card saying, "I love you more and more every day" can mean a lot; so, too, can an occasional phone call from work to say, "I miss you," or an affectionate note slipped surreptitiously into the family mailbox. A special dish or, if time permits, a special meal would make an equally nice surprise.

Trying to please each other in little things implies courtesy and consideration. If, while dating, the man was polite enough to pause before a meal so that his fiancée could be the first to start, if he held her coat for her or helped her into automobiles, then he should do the same as her husband. If, along parallel lines, she deferred to him in public and took pains to look her best, she can be sure that such things will continue to make him happy. Some of the social graces and amenities commonplace a generation or

---

[1] Cor. 11:3, 9; Col. 3:18; Titus 2:5; 1 Pet. 3:1-7. See also Genesis 2:18 and 3:16. *Arcanum Divinae Sapientiae* (1880) by Pope Leo XIII calls man "the ruler of the family." Pope Pius XI, in *Casti Connubii* (1930), quoted Pope Leo XIII and alluded to the husband's "chief place in ruling" (no. 2). According to the Catechism, man and woman were "created for one another," and each can be helpmate to the other; but woman was specially given by God to man "as a 'helpmate'" (no. 1605).

two ago may have vanished. But the general idea of courtship, whether in or out of marriage, remains as valid as ever.

Go out of your way to be positive. Refrain from reminiscing about old flames, and don't dignify temptations against the Sixth Commandment by confessing them to your spouse. Keep your eyes under control and your heart under strict lock and key at all times, striving for a loyalty that is one hundred percent. If, by chance, someone of the opposite sex should happen to attract you in a serious way, do not confide in such a person. Avoid unnecessary contact, and you'll be amazed at how quickly the problem disappears. You may not be doing anything that is technically wrong, but people are bound to talk, and such talk can spread. Discretion calls for the elimination of undue familiarity with anyone who could pose as a rival for your affection. As Father Frank Lee puts it, "Marriage does not simply bring two people together; it also excludes any third person. A word to the wise—everybody wants to be mature and sophisticated and modern and a few other big words, but we are still little human beings who are very jealous of our treasures."[2]

No Second Guessing

Imagine a home in which the husband forgets to put the cap back on his toothpaste after brushing. Time and again, she reminds him; time and again he forgets. Finally, one morning, she awakes to find the tube perfectly capped. He has mended his ways! But her first reaction is, "Honey, how come you aren't brushing your teeth anymore?" No one likes to be second-guessed.

Giving the Benefit of the Doubt

How would you react if you found yourself on the receiving end of a miscarriage, birth defect, or inability to conceive? Can there be any such thing as a "mistake" or misfortune when it

---

[2] Liguori Publications, Sunday flyer for December 28, 1975.

comes to products of divine engineering? Granted, it requires faith to accept what God sends, or fails to send, and to see in childlessness (or parenthood under difficult circumstances) a divinely appointed mission on a par with any other. But without such faith we fall prey to groundless feelings of guilt. Childlessness may involve some deficiency on the part of the woman, but there are times when it can be traced to the man. It is best, therefore, not to jump to conclusions. Even in situations where something or someone is clearly lacking, the partner who is truly in love will respond with the charity Saint Paul had in mind when he wrote that "love is patient and kind. . . . Love bears all things, believes all things, hopes all things, endures all things" (1 Cor. 13:4-7).

The Bible tells of an exemplary husband, Elkanah, whose barren wife, Hannah, was given to continual weeping over her condition. Elkanah could have compounded Hannah's grief by dismissing her. Instead, he pleads endearingly, "Am I not more to you than ten sons?" (1 Sam. 1:8). Elkanah and Hannah were eventually blessed with the birth of a son, Samuel, who went on to become one of the world's most celebrated prophets (cf. 1 Sam. 1:20), and other children as well (cf. 1 Sam. 2:21). Elkanah discovered that the Lord had a package on the shelf which He had delayed delivering, and there was ample reason to rejoice. Still, from the Christian standpoint, he was not so much released from sadness as simply introduced to a different kind of happiness with a whole new set of joys and sorrows, risks and responsibilities.

Right to Privacy

It may seem like a small point, but one can easily forget that married people have just as much of a right to privacy as anyone else. Even the most gregarious individual will appreciate a moment or two, now and then, to read, meditate, or simply to relax. Not all homes are spacious enough to afford a den or a sewing room, but there should be some kind of haven to which one can retreat without fear of intrusion. It might even be a desk or a sofa, as long as it is viewed as "off limits" when certain persons occupy it at certain times. The amazing thing is that children can be just as cooperative in this regard as grown-ups once they understand the reason why.

Youngsters and Discipline

Not surprisingly, it is the little ones who tend to be most malleable. From the moment of birth, they are gifted with a quite remarkable sense of right and wrong, and you will find that, with persistence on your part, along with a reasonable system of rewards and punishments, they take rather well to discipline, at times almost demanding it. Aside from food and rest, children are hungry for two things above all else: discipline and affection, and they need them in equal proportion. If they are not kissed, held, hugged, indulged on occasion, and listened to, they will find it hard to obey; and if they don't obey, they won't remain huggable or kissable for long. Appearances notwithstanding, each of them, deep down, also likes to be told in a tactful way what to do and how to do it. Gradually, and with patience, they can be taught to behave with restraint, courtesy, and consideration, and when this happens, they add immeasurably to the joy of home life. If, on the other hand, they are permitted to roam and rummage at will, to jump, scream, and disturb the neighbors, if their unruliness begins to drive a wedge between the parties responsible for their welfare, as it surely will, they will be the first to suffer.

A smooth-running household coupled with proper management of the children is integral to the whole notion of Christian generosity in procreation. How can parents be disposed to welcome more children if those already on board are a constant nuisance? How can they make time for a larger family if their daily schedule is already a shambles or if their lines of communication have broken down?

Since every child is unique, the key to wholesome discipline lies in knowing what to expect from each as an individual and taking the time to find out. Obviously, they should not be punished for doing what they cannot help or for failing to measure up to an unreasonably high standard. Infants with severe gastrointestinal pain are going to cry; babies, when they teethe, are going to drool—some of them like Niagara Falls! But it is never a mistake to aim high. Experienced parents know how often youngsters are likely to surprise them by accomplishing the "impossible."

As to method, most would agree that corporal punishment should be held to a minimum. Some children are so docile that an occasional verbal reprimand is all they need. For the majority, however, a timely slap on the hand or a spanking administered dispassionately will do a world of good.

"Spare the rod and spoil the child," one of the better-known precepts drawn from Scripture (cf. Prov. 13:24), was embellished in a humorous vein by the late Archbishop Fulton Sheen, who quipped, "No child is ever hurt by an occasional pat on the back as long as it is given low enough and hard enough." Clearly, there are limits to what can be achieved under any system. Too much punishment may be worse than none at all. At the same time, one seldom hears an adult taking his parents to task for having been too strict, assuming they were conscientious and set a good example. Dwight D. Eisenhower grew up in a family of six boys. All were exposed to the often erratic temper and leather strap of a strict father. Yet there was not a single black sheep in the fold.

One of the most positive techniques is to have children help out around the house so they can learn the value of honest work and experience the joy of giving. At the earliest age, they are incredibly eager to be helpful, perhaps sensing the relationship between work and maturity. Whatever the reason, a skillful parent will foster this eagerness by assigning appropriate tasks and taking time to encourage children in their effort.

Finally, because parents represent the justice, as well as the mercy, of God, it behooves them to be truthful and to avoid even the appearance of favoritism. At the same time, by agreeing privately on matters of discipline, they will avoid the temptation to fight and countermand each other's orders before the children. Remember that children, always quick to find chinks in the parental armor, can be mercilessly exploitative.

The Beauty of Schedules

You may be one of those who are temperamentally averse to any form of structure or regimentation. But if you are open to suggestion along this line, there is much to be said for family routine. If nothing else, it maximizes the time at your disposal and gives everyone a heightened sense of belonging. As long as mealtime is anyone's guess and the whereabouts of family members a mystery, there is bound to be some lag in morale. Conversely, when a definite time is set aside for dinner, as well as for cleaning, laundry, shopping, church-going, and family outings, young and old will be able to plan accordingly. Children, especially, will benefit from having a regular schedule if they are to complete their homework, attend to chores, and say their prayers. I can still remember how happy our daughter Mary Anne was at the age of four when we invited her to join us in saying the last decade of the evening Rosary. Thereafter, at exactly the appointed time, she wanted nothing so much as to set up the holy card along with the beads, and watch the candle being lit. In fact, she would remind us if we forgot!

The more children there are at home, the greater the need to ensure that each of them receives a daily quota of "quality time." Those of school age will be fortunate if they are limited in their access to TV. They will also have set bed times, along with sufficient exercise during the day to keep them in a prone position at night.

When all is said and done, personal sacrifice is the glue that is going to hold your brood together. Once you march down that aisle, consider yourself more or less on permanent duty. It may be tempting to dodge family cares for a while and go off on your own. You may even be tempted to run home, ostrich-like, to father and mother. But prudence dictates otherwise. Everyone benefits from an occasional time-out, and if you can afford babysitting, or if there is someone trustworthy who is willing to spell you, then by all means escape. But the children will be grown before you know it and, in the early stages, they stand to benefit enormously from every moment you spend with them. I needn't add that when you and your partner do go away, it is advisable to spend the time together. Separate vacations are not, on the whole, very constructive.

Budgeting

Your goal here should be to save as much as you can for education and retirement. Such prudence will serve as a hedge against sudden illness while leaving the door open to generosity in matters of procreation. If husband and wife both have a career outside the home and it seems advisable for one of them to leave full-time work (or quit altogether) so that he or she can assume primary care of the children, this ought to be encouraged. In no case should the "homemaker" spouse be *forced* to work outside the home. Such a decision, if taken, should be taken jointly, and the work should be such that it can be scaled back or discontinued in the event that it poses a threat to the family. Based on Christian principles, it is far better to live with only two or three outfits in one's closet than to short-change those whose lifelong welfare depends in so many instances on our watchful presence.

The actual budget takes time, but it is not all that difficult and will repay all the effort you put into it. First, jot down your fixed expenses for the year. For example: rent or mortgage payments, insurance premiums, telephone bills, automobile depreciation, utilities, taxes, haircuts, cleaners, laundry, and cosmetics. Items like rent, which are normally calculated on a monthly basis, should be multiplied by twelve to arrive at the annual cost. There may be other regular items depending on your situation (visits to the dentist or eye doctor, transportation to work, and so forth). Charitable contributions, along with outlays for the support of the parish, should be at the very top of one's list of "fixed" expenses. Anyone who can afford a pizza or a movie once in a while can drop at least this much into the collection basket on Sunday. Remember the parable of the widow's mite (Mk. 12:41-44). You will find it useful, in addition, to have a category called "miscellaneous," still under the heading of fixed expenses. This will allow for freak occurrences such as emergency repairs and replacement of appliances. Expect the unexpected, and budget for it.

Next draw up a list of flexible items, again figuring on a twelve-month basis: food, clothing, savings, recreation, entertainment, vacations, magazine and newspaper subscriptions, gifts, and the like. If, after adding up all the expenses on both lists, you find that a single income is insufficient, you should begin paring down the figures on each list, especially on the second list, until you arrive at a satisfactory balance.

As we all know, the best way to save is to not spend, which means purchasing only what is absolutely necessary at reasonable prices. If you are the type who cannot resist bargains unrelated to immediate family needs, bring an itemized list to the supermarket to avoid impulse buying. Otherwise, you will be on the road to the poor house. Beware of installment plans. No one can ever be sure what kind of demand the future is going to make on a family's income. Many who rely on credit wind up paying exorbitant sums of interest for the privilege of deferring payment on goods they should never have bought in the first place. Look out, too, for "Ma Bell." She can kill you by turning 35¢ into $35 when you are not looking. Be sure also to use a checkbook. Balance it every month and pay by check as often as possible, especially when purchasing substantial items. In this way, you'll have an itemized record of where your money is going when it comes time to plan next year's budget. Save bank and credit card statements for a full year, if possible, and cancelled checks for ten. You never know when you may need to produce them for insurance purposes or the IRS.

As for who holds the purse strings, they should be jointly held in most cases. Congenital spendthrifts exist, but they are rare. Likewise when it comes to deciding how to dispose of family income. The mere fact that you are bound by a budget will render certain decisions automatic, and the ones that are not should be subject to compromise based on who feels more strongly. If each party bends a little, neither will be on the losing end. Most of the time, when finances pose a serious problem, the source of the difficulty can be traced to a lack of love.

In-Laws

However much two families may have in common, they will not react to all situations in exactly the same way any more than they will share the same expectations. On a purely practical level, they are likely to have different ways of celebrating religious feasts and holidays. Feelings can run deep as to how many presents should be exchanged at Christmas and when they should be opened. Familiarity breeds contempt, and parents of the bride and groom, while not intending it, can easily come between husband and wife.

Don't misunderstand. Some couples, when they marry, develop a wonderful relationship with their new families. Grandparents are a godsend. They can be extremely generous. And who can forget the story of Ruth, an Old Testament widow, who assured her mother-in-law that "where you go I will go, and where you lodge I will lodge; your people shall be my people, and your God my God" (Ruth 1:16). In-laws deserve the greatest respect and consideration. At the very least, we should avoid criticizing them, especially in the presence of our mate, when in doing so we may be treading on a loyalty that is as deeply rooted as it is natural. Even if the criticism strikes a sympathetic chord, it will put one's partner in an awkward spot.

At the same time, it has been well said that "in-laws are out-laws." Like all adages, this one may not ring entirely true in every instance, but it contains a wealth of wisdom. Scripture has it that "a man leaves his father and his mother and cleaves to his wife, and they become one flesh" (Gen. 2:24). Therefore, in any dispute pitting spouse against in-law (or blood relative, for that matter), the spouse's mate should remain neutral or, preferably, come down on the side of his or her partner. Likewise, if a parent requires correction, the person to do it is the blood relative. We are enjoined by the Fourth Commandment to honor father and mother, but our primary allegiance is to the person we marry, and couples who experience friction with their relatives are advised to limit the contact. If and when in-laws offer advice, the prudent response is, "Thank you for your thoughtfulness; I'll talk it over with my better half." Never complain, and never tolerate remarks or behavior from family members that denigrate your spouse, even indirectly. As mentioned earlier, smooth communication between husband and wife is essential to the health of the marriage, and this calls for one hundred percent loyalty.

Family Friends

When it comes to friends, it is well to adopt a similar attitude, subordinating personal attachments to the larger goal of a secure and happy home. Following the wedding, one or both spouses may have to forge new ties if they find their partner ill at ease with long-time associates or, as sometimes happens, overly fond of them.

Friendship between married couples can be an especially difficult proposition since all four of the spouses must like, or at least not dislike, each spouse of the other couple; and along with the liking, there must be an absence of romantic attachment. Generally speaking, the friends you cultivate should share your underlying values. Christian hospitality has a place, and good fellowship is again something to be cherished, but neither has anything to do with opening your home to people whose behavior is scandalous or whose offspring may prejudice your family's chance to mature in an environment that is morally safe and culturally stimulating.[3]

The Children's Education

Parents have the right, as well as the duty, to educate their children, especially in matters of faith and morals.[4] This calls for perpetual vigilance with respect to TV, film, and theater programs, many of which are slanted in such a way as to undermine the Catholic ideal of marriage. When they are not downright filthy, they often present abortion, adultery, and remarriage after divorce as perfectly acceptable, if not praiseworthy.

Another responsibility that is part and parcel of Catholic parenting is the fostering of religious vocations. This is not something that can be left to chance. If good priests and nuns, sisters and brothers, are not included in the family circle of friends, how are youngsters to find religious role models? How often, in our secular, materialistic culture, do we hear the frivolous parental boast that little Johnny, at the age of five, "has a girlfriend"? This is a perfect example of what *not* to do. According to Vatican II, "parents should beware of exercising any undue influence, directly or indirectly, to force them into marriage or compel them in their choice of partners" (GS 52).

Responsible parenthood also calls for the placing of children in a wholesome intellectual environment commensurate with their ability. Most importantly, it means making sure that they receive the right instruction in such Christian virtues as modesty,

---

[3] See Appendix B.
[4] GE 3. According to the Catechism, parents, not the state, "have the primary responsibility for the procreation and education of their children" (no. 2372). They are "the principal and first educators of their children," and "the fundamental task of marriage and family is to be at the service of life" (no. 1653). Parents also have the right to choose a school for their offspring "which corresponds to their own convictions" (no. 2229).

temperance, and purity. It is far more important that they turn out to be men and women of character than that they be erudite, even though the two goals can be mutually reinforcing. There is a tendency to assume that, when youngsters are sent off to Catholic schools, they will receive all that they need in this area. But not necessarily. It all depends on the institution. Some Catholic schools and colleges do an excellent job of instructing students in the fundamentals of their faith. Others do not. Consequently, parents must be well informed about the school curriculum in order to supplement or counteract it when necessary. It goes without saying that the ideal place for sons and daughters to learn "the facts of life" is at home, where their teachers, Mom and Dad, practice what they preach. But if it has to be at school, one should know precisely what is being taught and how. In certain situations, one may even have to go a step further and request that a child be excused from class.

In recent years, the moral caliber of public, and even private, education has declined sharply, and an increasing number of families have turned to home schooling. Not every parent is properly equipped for this kind of work—it is difficult under the best of circumstances. On the other hand, there is much to be said for a system that affords such a high degree of control over content, as well as a merciful side-stepping of astronomical tuition bills. There are also some very good programs available complete with texts, workbooks, parent manuals, and telephone hot lines (see Appendix M).

A Bright and Cheerful Home

Shifting the focus for just a moment, you have undoubtedly thought about the kind of home you want—one that is bright, clean, and reasonably in order, as well as comfortable and inviting to members of the family. There is no need for slavish imitation of all the stylish models featured in picture magazines. But there are things one can do by way of decoration and furnishing to make the place where you live "Home, Sweet Home." As far as personal appearance is concerned, a moment or two before the mirror, now and then, will be time well spent. A quick touch of the comb, an occasional dash of cold water on the face, or a fresh outfit will add to the domestic ambiance, and this goes for both spouses. To be sure, home is a place to relax and unwind. But it should also be a pleasant place, cozy enough for family members to miss when they are away for any length of time.

Poverty, Chastity, and Obedience

Doubtless you are familiar with the three vows taken by men and women who enter the religious life: poverty, chastity, and obedience. But have you ever considered that these same requirements govern the lives of those who are married?

Chastity, not to be confused with virginity or celibacy, is a matter of keeping one's sexual appetite under control within the limits set by God. As such, it is likely to pose as much of a challenge to the married person as it does to the nun or priest. In marriage, such factors as physical absence, pregnancy, lack of privacy, domestic strife, and even nervous exhaustion can be formidable barriers to self-expression and therefore to chastity. Celibacy, on the other hand, which calls for constant restraint, may be less difficult precisely because it is constant.

Chastity calls for modesty in dress and behavior, just as it excludes anything that might give rise to scandal or lead to an adulterous relationship. Clearly, there are many ways of sinning against the Sixth Commandment: by what one says, by one's body language, and by what one communicates through the eyes (cf. Mt. 5:28). In Leo Tolstoy's masterpiece, *Anna Karenina*, an attractive young woman (Anna), who is married to an elder statesman, decides to travel some distance in order to help her brother put his affairs in order. En route, at a railway station, she catches sight of a dashing young army officer by the name of

Vronsky. Turning on the platform to give him a second look, she commits a fatal indiscretion, for in that split second, a romantic attachment is conceived which leads to the birth of an illegitimate child. In the end, a desperately unhappy Anna throws herself in the path of an oncoming steam locomotive.

The prudent spouse will consider whether lunch with a business associate of the opposite sex has to be a private affair or whether it can be arranged as more of an official function in an impersonal setting. There will also be times when one's daily routine may call for adjustment in order to avoid a too friendly colleague, knowing that one thing can lead to another.

In short, prudence and discretion are golden in marriage just as they are in the religious life. Shakespeare's play, *Othello*, focuses on the machinations of the wicked Iago, who manages to convince Othello that the latter's wife, Desdemona, has been unfaithful with Cassio. Desdemona may be innocent, but she is also imprudent, for on her honeymoon no less, she prods Othello to reinstate Cassio, thereby fueling her husband's suspicion. It makes no difference that her solicitude for Cassio springs from unselfish motives. She has been indiscreet, and it is the indiscretion that seals her fate.

Poverty, second of the three vows, has less to do with some federally designated minimum standard of living than with a Christlike spirit of detachment. How much in the way of material goods does one need to be happy? The more possessions we have, the more we worry, and the more complicated our life becomes. Imposing homes and costly appointments, because they require continual care, can place heavy demands on our limited store of time and energy. Tolstoy's short story, "How Much Land Does a Man Need?" tells of a man who spends every waking moment of his life acquiring real estate. On reaching a certain section of the country, he is told that for a given sum he can secure title to all the land he is able to stake out on foot in a single day. Pleased, he starts off early in the morning at a frenzied pace, darting here and there to lay claim to the choicest parcels. As the sun begins to set, however, he is still far afield with much unfinished business, and in one last, desperate effort to complete his survey, he collapses from sheer exhaustion and falls dead at the feet of the owners, who promptly dig him a hole six-feet deep by three-feet wide.

How much land does a man need? Christian detachment calls for a life of simplicity in keeping with the station to which one is called. Simplicity, in turn, opens the door to generosity. I shall never forget the title of a sermon I once saw posted outside a small church in Manhattan: "To Live Simply That Others May Simply Live."

One way of practicing economy is to refrain from impulse buying. Some couples seem to feel they must furnish their home all at once. Why so? By waiting for sales and shopping at a more leisurely pace, one will have a better sense of what is available, and the pieces that turn up along the way may be more to one's liking. Tastes and needs can change, and if our friends think less of us for living modestly, then perhaps we should find some new friends.

Obedience, the third vow, implies a readiness to yield in matters of personal preference, and it applies as much to the home as it does to the rectory. It has little to do with playing doormat and everything to do with Christian deference. Does your mate feel strongly about a particular charitable cause? Then contribute. Does your partner have a better sense of where to hang pictures? Be grateful. And if you are the one with the better sense, you can still go along in the interest of tranquility. Does your spouse complain about being lonely or neglected? Perhaps your job is working too much of a hardship on the home. It may be time to rearrange your schedule or find a new position. All of us are obliged to do an honest day's work for an honest day's pay. In fact, it is our Christian *duty* to excel in every way possible. But having said this, we must not forget that the welfare of our family comes first, and conjugal obedience means doing whatever it takes to foster a spirit of husbandly and wifely solicitude.

The Missionary Spirit

It is easy to overlook the importance of the ordinary home as a missionary outpost. We live in a world controlled by skeptics and non-believers, and although history testifies to prodigious feats of conversion accomplished in faraway places such as India, Africa, and Latin America, there is an urgent need for missionaries here at home. Today's "heathen" are more apt to be rich than poor, educated than uneducated. Many of them attend Sunday Mass out of a knee-jerk respect for tradition or ethnic ritual, and we may be the only serious Catholics they ever meet. Uninformed when it comes to Church teaching, they pick and choose, cafeteria style, among various rules and precepts. Some will tell you that it doesn't really matter what one believes so long as one is "sincere." Poor souls. They need to ask themselves why Jesus died, why He commissioned the apostles to preach to all nations, and why thousands of Christians in every age have sacrificed their lives for what they believed.

Vatican II stressed that if we are to offer an example of family living that is wholesome, if we are to advertise our love for Jesus, if we are going to answer questions that come our way, we must familiarize ourselves with the fundamentals of the faith on an adult level. This could call for attendance at a Bible class, for more regular reading and meditation on Sacred Scripture, or for dipping more deeply into the lives of the martyrs and saints. Another approach might be to subscribe to Catholic newspapers and magazines. When religious instruction terminates at the age of twelve or thirteen, as is generally the case, one may boast all one wants of a college education; but in the area that counts most, one continues to function at an elementary school level. Religious education is a continual, lifelong process.

Returning, though, to the domestic front: Will TV be enshrined as the high altar of your home? Will you select a *Playboy* air freshener for your car or something more in keeping with what you profess to believe? A friend of mine used to have a tiny cactus on his desk as a reminder of Christ's crown of thorns, one of many ways he had hit upon to stay in touch with reality.

We should ask ourselves how guests are going to know that ours is a Catholic home and that we care about the salvation of souls. Will their eyes be drawn to a crucifix or some other object of religious art that has special meaning for us?

How will you and your family celebrate Sundays and holy days? Will they be different from regular days in the sense of avoiding unnecessary shopping and employment? Is Mass going to be something to be gotten out of the way as quickly as possible, with your troop arriving late in cutoffs and sneakers and then leaving early, or will you be prepared physically, mentally, and spiritually for God's Eucharistic banquet? Will Easter be reduced to chocolate eggs and bunnies, or will there be some reminder of the Christian dimension? How do you propose to reflect on the meaning of the Cross and Resurrection? In short, how are you going to "keep the faith" and foster religious vocations, a responsibility that rests as much with the laity as it does with nuns and priests?

Will you keep a small library of spiritual classics side-by-side with the Bible, and will your children have access to inspirational works suitable for their age? Ignatius Press and the Daughters of St. Paul have published some excellent volumes on the lives of the saints. Highly recommended, too, is *The Imitation of Christ* by Thomas á Kempis, *Introduction to the Devout and Holy Life* by Saint Francis de Sales, and *The Way* by Blessed Josemaría Escrivá de Balaguer. Fulton Oursler and Archbishop Fulton Sheen wrote first-rate biographies of Christ. What one reads has much to do with what kind of person one is, as well as with the type of person one is likely to become.

Chapter 4
Spirituality

When one hears the familiar words, "for better or for worse, for richer or for poorer, in sickness and in health," one tends to think of material concerns, the ups and downs of the stock market, or a bout with the flu. But another, more significant side of these vows is their supernatural content. There will be "dark nights of the soul." In the end, God will ask each of us if we have made it easier or harder for our spouse to get to heaven, and as a consequence, we need to be spiritually involved.

Spirituality is a hard word to define. I remember one of my college roommates saying that he would like to marry a saint. When I asked him why, he replied that a saint is a person who is not only happy but also capable of making others happy. At the time, his words were simply words—I had only the vaguest sense of what he was driving at. Today, though, after having pulled in harness with a sterling partner for over thirty years, I can appreciate something of the clarity of his vision.

Many of the world's greatest saints were in fact married, among them Thomas More of England, Louis IX of France, Monica (mother of Saint Augustine), Margaret Clitherow of York, Isidore of Madrid, Margaret of Scotland, and Frances of Rome, not to mention the Holy Family and John the Baptist's parents, Zechariah and Elizabeth. So there is no dearth of role models.

Saints are not born; they are made, many of them later in life. If one reads the story of Saint Augustine or Saint Ignatius of Loyola, one finds both of them wayward as young men, but once they experienced the saving grace of conversion, they sped upward at a breathtaking pace to the very pinnacle of perfection. Was it easy? Saint Paul likens the quest for Christian perfection to the running of a race, and races are exhausting (cf. 1 Cor. 9:24; 2 Tim. 4:7). But if devotees of physical fitness can engage in aerobics, jogging, dieting, and body building at all hours of the day and night, why shouldn't we go out of our way to do some of the things recommended for fitness of the soul?

Neither my wife nor I would ever claim to be saints. Far from it. Traveling together on life's journey, we can look back on our share of flat tires. The Lord has had to put up with an awful lot from me in particular, and He still does. It is just that the two of us have been on the road long enough to know that there are a number of practical, down-to-earth measures which can help a family stay the course, and the first of these is prayer.

Prayer

Exxon Corporation used to advertise its brand of gasoline as one that would "put a tiger in your tank." We, too, need to put a tiger in our tank, and one of the ways of doing this, I have found, is through prayer.

Motoring through some of the rural areas of Ohio, my wife and I used to see billboards with a homey message: "The family that prays together stays together." It struck a sympathetic chord because we knew it to be true. Christ said the same thing, of course, when He promised that "every one who asks receives" and "where two or three are gathered in my name, there am I in the midst of them" (Mt. 7:8; 18:20). With God, all things are possible, provided they are pleasing in His sight, and one of the most pleasing is a love affair between a man and a woman that never ends.

When the priest asked Johnny if he said his prayers every night before going to bed, Johnny responded, "Yes, Father." "And do you also say them when you wake up in the morning?" continued the padre. "No, Father." "And why not, Johnny?" Came the confident answer: " 'Cause I ain't never scared during the day!" All of us have a bit of the Johnny in us. We fall to our knees on the death of a sweetheart or at the onset of terminal cancer, and the rest of the time we are content to coast. We forget that it is the events of everyday life that make or break a marriage, and that the same source of strength invoked in times of extreme difficulty is available to us every day of the week.

Most of us pray at set times such as early in the morning, at mealtime, and again before turning in. Without question, such prayer—call it formal prayer, if you will—can be rewarding. At the same time, there is something to be said for praying in a less formal manner. Not that one approach precludes the other. On the contrary, Saint Paul tells us to pray "at all times" (Eph. 6:18; 1 Thess. 5:17), which means that we should learn to engage in heavenly chit-chat while mowing the lawn and doing the dishes.

A typical conversation might go something like this: "Well, Lord, here I am again rocking the baby on my chest and applying hot compresses to her aching ear. She's in such pain! But I know that You're there and won't abandon us. I know, too, that You'll have other assignments for me. Can You see the smile on my face? It makes me happy to think that all of this is for You." Or suppose you're in a traffic jam and you exclaim, "Lord, what a mess! I'm not complaining, but why have You got me sandwiched in here bumper-to-bumper? Because You miss hearing from me on normal occasions? Is there something deep down in my life that needs correcting? Aha. So that's it!"

Saint Teresa of Avila, as jolly a soul as ever lived, traveled the highways and byways of Spain on any number of occasions, all in the service of God. Transportation was primitive in those days, and once, after her carriage overturned crossing a stream, she burst out, "Lord, if this is the way you treat your friends, no wonder you have so few of them!" Like Teresa, we should go to God as we are, thinking about all that He has reserved for us in heaven and jotting down some of the things we plan to do when we get there.

Prayer can have interesting side effects. As a writer, I used to be annoyed by library patrons who coughed with such maddening regularity that it seemed they wanted everyone in the room to notice them. On other occasions, I was galled by the sound of car alarms going off under my office window. The only solution that worked, I found, was to say a Hail Mary every time I heard a cough or car alarm. Let me tell you, no church bell or Angelus could have been more effective as a call to meditation. And with what results! Not only did my prayer life improve, my writing perked up, my spirits revived, and I soon reached the point of looking forward to the next interruption! Just think how different life would be if the average supermarket clerk or toll collector in large, impersonal cities like New York, where rudeness is the rule, came to view everyday work as their ticket to heaven, rather than as a form of drudgery. In place of sourpusses, we would have a legion of smiling angels.

The application to marriage should be clear. Prayer is a form of communication, and once we learn to communicate with God, we will be that much more effective at reaching our spouse. If nothing else, the two indispensable phrases, "I love you" and "I'm sorry," will be quicker to roll off our lips because we will be saying them over and over to the Lord.

The Sacraments

Next to prayer, and just as important for keeping a "tiger in the tank," are three very special sacraments: Penance (the Sacrament of Reconciliation or Confession), Holy Communion, and Matrimony itself. Together, they open the floodgates of a spiritual reservoir from which one can draw down inexhaustible energy and inspiration.

Matrimony

Matrimony, to begin in reverse order, is more than a contract in which bride and groom pledge themselves to each other for better or worse. It is also a solemn covenant between the couple and God, as well as between the couple and society. As such, it carries with it a mighty reserve of spiritual power to assist us in the discharge of our conjugal duties. Fortunately, such grace, conferred during the wedding ceremony, remains a constant source of strength throughout married life.

Scripture vividly tells us of the importance Christ attached to marriage. He likened His kingdom to a marriage feast, chose a wedding celebration at Cana as the occasion for His first public miracle, and selected a humble family to be the instrument of His salvation. God could have come to us in a variety of ways. What is remarkable is that He chose to come through the womb of a woman and was raised, like any other child, by a father and mother. Presumably, Mary did the laundry and diapers, along with the cooking, as was customary at the time. In addition, Jesus' respect for marriage was such that He impressed upon His followers the revolutionary principle of indissolubility, declaring that "what God has joined together" let "no man put asunder." Matthew, Mark, Luke, and Paul all indicate, beyond any reasonable doubt, that Our Lord was unconditional in forbidding remarriage after divorce.[1]

Reconciliation

It hardly seems possible that mere mortals could possess the power to confer God's pardon. Yet Christ told Peter and the other apostles as a group: "If you forgive the sins of any, they are forgiven; if you retain the sins of any, they are retained" (Jn. 20:23).

Confession calls for courage on the part of the penitent, but how exhilarating it is to know that one has been made clean in the eyes of God! Among nonbelievers, some are so enamored of reconciliation as a sacrament that they regard it as the most appealing feature of Catholicism. Psychiatrists, too, have long recognized its utility as a means of removing guilt. Indeed, it is curious that people will pay for the privilege of reclining on a doctor's couch when they can go to Confession without charge. Perhaps they stay away

---

[1] See Appendix B.

from the confessional because they know the priest will echo Christ's command to the woman caught in adultery: "go, and do not sin again" (Jn. 8:11). Yet this is precisely what they are most in need of hearing. Just as an automobile requires periodic oil changes to lubricate its moving parts and improve performance, so too, in the case of the soul. We need to have our "spiritual fluids" refreshed from time to time if we are to avoid a build-up of the kind of moral sludge that erodes the joy of conscious integrity and hampers our relations with others.

There should be ample opportunity for Confession at neighborhood churches. But in an emergency, anyone can walk into any Catholic rectory at any time, ask for help, and normally the priest will be happy to oblige.

Hell

It is not fashionable in today's topsy-turvy world to dwell on the torments of hell. But the truth of the matter is that damnation is mentioned dozens of times in the Bible. Christ Himself described it as "everlasting fire" where there is "the weeping and gnashing of teeth," a phrase that appears no less than four times in the Gospel of Matthew alone.

The point to bear in mind is that there are two kinds of sin: mortal and venial. Mortal sin, the more serious of the two, bars us from Holy Communion and consigns us to hell unless we go to Confession or make a perfect act of contrition on our deathbed. However, in order for a sin to be mortal, it has to meet three criteria:

1. It must be a serious matter.
2. We must be aware of its seriousness.
3. We must act with full consent of the will—that is to say, we must know exactly what we are doing, be fully aware of the consequences, and freely act with full deliberation (Catechism, nos. 1857-59).

If any one of these conditions is absent, the sin in question is venial, and we are not obliged to confess it. One hastens to add, however, that even venial sin is an affront to God, and as such, *we are urged not to take such offenses lightly.* All too often, when we don't aim at perfection as Christ recommended (cf. Mt. 5:48), we find ourselves sliding in the opposite direction.

One or two examples will suffice to illustrate the difference between venial and mortal sin. Let us assume, for the sake of argument, that we are with friends and the talk turns suggestive or verges on malicious gossip. We are taken by surprise, and before we know it, an off-color joke has drawn laughs or someone's reputation has been dragged through the mud. We may feel mean for not having tried to change the subject, but we have not sinned mortally because the thing we did, or failed to do, was unintentional. If, on the other hand, we and our partner (a) have chosen to live together as man and wife before marriage; (b) realize that the Church views such conduct as a serious offense against God; and (c) in spite of knowing that the Church enjoins us to call a halt, see a priest, confess, and carry out the prescribed penance, we insist on going our way, we are in a state of mortal sin.

As a rule, we are apt to find one sin particularly hard to root out, and this can be discouraging. Returning again and again to the confessional with the same old story can seem pointless, if not self-defeating. Yet isn't this what one does on the physical level to fight disease? Do we not take antibiotics over and over again? Does a cancer patient not submit to repeated radiation as part of chemotherapy? If we were to go after moral cancer with the same kind of determination, could we not expect similar results? Interior change takes time, but God will not deny us the power we need if we ask for it often enough and indicate at each step along the way a willingness to do our part. Christ came on earth to conquer sin, and He will give us the grace we need to conquer ourselves if we receive the Sacrament of Penance with a firm purpose of amendment, coupled with a practical plan of reform.

Here again, there is a direct application to the married state, for to seek reconciliation with God by facing our shortcomings and doing so regularly, say at least once a month, is to cultivate humility, and it is this virtue, more than any other, that will enable us to remain cheerful in moments of distress and yield on matters of personal preference.

Communion

A good Confession is like a good shower after days of personal neglect. It spruces us up and paves the way for a worthy reception of Holy Communion, the third of the spiritual resources recommended for couples seeking to keep their love alive and fresh. Those who receive Our Lord's body and blood avail themselves of the greatest privilege known to man, something so mystical and awesome that it caused many of Christ's followers to break with Him because they could not believe He was serious when He said, "unless you eat the flesh of the Son of man and drink his blood, you have no life in you. . . . For my flesh is food indeed, and my blood is drink indeed" (Jn. 6:53-55). Note that Jesus insisted on a literal interpretation of these words when He let the malcontents go rather than offer further explanation (Jn. 6:60-66).

Our Lord knew something that we humans have a tendency to forget: namely, that the soul needs sustenance as much as the body if it is to retain a sense of well-being, and the Eucharist is the most nourishing of all foods. There have always been those who claim that it is sufficient for them to pray at home and perform good works. What about regular churchgoers, they ask, who are anything but God-fearing on the other six days of the week? Appearances can be deceptive, however. Studies indicate that those who attend church regularly are more than twice as likely to remain married as their stay-at-home brethren. They are also apt to live longer, have fewer heart attacks, and experience a lower incidence of hypertension, arteriosclerosis, and high blood pressure. Equally to the point, a 1990 Gallup poll indicates that they give four times as much to charity and volunteer twice as much of their time. They are nearly twice as likely to donate to nonreligious charities, and if one credits *The New York Times*, they are much less likely to cheat on their income tax.[2]

With a certain amount of preparation beforehand and a sincere act of thanksgiving afterward, reception of Christ's body and blood helps us subdue our carnal appetites. This is important because, contrary to the popular impression, marriage does not shield us from temptation. Whether single or married, we must strive resolutely to drive out impure thoughts and exercise self-control.

Fasting and Abstinence

One of the best methods of staying spiritually fit, as well as preparing for Communion, is to fast and abstain from choice foods as a symbol of the sorrow that we feel, or *ought* to feel, for our many sins.[3] Such a practice used to be mandatory on Fridays. Today, one is permitted to substitute some other kind of mortification (cf. Catechism, no. 1438). But there is still plenty of room for the method recommended by Jesus, Peter, John, and Paul (Mt. 6:17-18, 9:14-15; 1 Pet. 2:11; 1 Cor. 9:27). Just as it is wise, when one drives an automobile on ice, to apply the brakes every so often just to make sure one is in control, so too, when it comes to the "braking" of the body. Life is slippery and the body treacherous. We want to be sure we are in control in times of temptation. Fasting is also the road to humility. It reminds us of who we are and whom we serve, just as it reinforces our willingness to sacrifice when our lives are difficult. A family that goes without dessert on Friday is also in a position to donate the amount they save to a favorite charity, thus enhancing the benefit to all.

---

[2] *The New York Times* (April 20, 1991), 10; Yancey, "God is Good for You," 1-2; *National Catholic Register* (May 24, 1992), 5. See also Appendix D.

[3] According to the Catechism, "There is no holiness without renunciation and spiritual battle" (no. 2015).

Apostolic Zeal

Thus far, we have focused on the effect of deepening religious commitment on conjugal relations. True spirituality, however, operates on an extremely broad front, reaching out to friends, relatives, neighbors, and the world at large in accord with Jesus' command: "as you did it to one of the least of these brethren, you did it to me" (Mt. 25:40). As in the game of volleyball, if you don't serve you can't win. We may be too busy to chauffeur a handicapped person to church or to baby-sit for someone who might otherwise have to miss Sunday Mass. Perhaps we find ourselves under too much pressure to lector, teach catechism, or help the pastor with a paint job. Will we then have a stack of postcards handy to contact the sponsors of TV programs, indicating support or voicing concern as the case may be?

In other words, what form will our charity take? Are we prepared to speak out on such issues as abortion and premarital sex? Have we studied controversial topics in the light of Church teaching? Are we ready to support couples whose matrimonial bonds show signs of snapping? Do we tell them, when they come to us in trouble, that we will gladly help them put their marriages back together again, but we won't help to tear them apart?

Our work itself can be tremendously fruitful as a means of sanctification, not only for ourselves but for those around us, provided we labor cheerfully and to the best of our ability, and that we are prepared to take risks. A lawyer friend of mine once remarked that when clients came to him for advice about initiating divorce proceedings, he would do all he could to save the marriage, even if it meant loss of income. Accountants who refuse to engage in deliberate falsification of figures may find themselves in the same situation. Oftentimes, there is a price to be paid for discipleship. But from a spiritual point of view, any losses we may incur are greatly outweighed by the gains.

Spirituality, like sunshine, casts its rays in every direction and over all sectors of life, whether they be professional, domestic, or recreational. Take something as mundane as a family trip. It will be more rewarding if, in addition to the usual tourist attractions, one takes in an occasional site of religious significance. Obviously, you will stop in Paris if you visit France. But those who go out of their way to include Lourdes on the itinerary will be deeply touched. Just as one would target the Holy Land on a trip to the Middle East, or the Vatican if one's destination were Italy, how could one leave Portugal without making a pilgrimage to Fatima, site of the most spectacular and thoroughly authenticated of all miracles? In our own hemisphere, on the outskirts of Mexico City, we are fortunate to have the Shrine of Our Lady of Guadalupe. As at Lourdes and Fatima, visitors to Guadalupe will be profoundly moved by their proximity to a miracle, for which the evidence is once again overwhelming. And what if you are planning a trip closer to home? There will be Catholic churches along the way, some of them attractive, some of them less so, but all of them houses of God. So why not drop in, from time to time, and spend a moment before the tabernacle to keep that conversation with Jesus going? What could be more refreshing?

I realize that such recommendations may sound like a tall order, especially when all of them are lumped together. But remember, they are merely suggestions. The only really serious mistake one can make in connection with spirituality is to underrate its importance.

When You Pray

One last thought about prayer: when you lift up your voice to heaven, don't expect God to return a booming response. At times, the silence from on high can be almost deafening! But keep on praying. He will answer in one form or another, even if it takes time. And if His answer turns out to be "No," you can be sure that, like any other responsible parent, He has His reasons. His message may come in the form of a coincidence that sets us thinking or even in the guise of trials and tribulations that present new prospects.

How would you react if you found that you could not have all the children you wanted? Would it surprise you if this were God's way of intimating that He had something else in mind for you, something different but just as worthwhile? Perhaps He wants you to spend a portion of your time ministering to the needs of other families. Assuming your spouse is agreeable, you might opt for adoption or devote yourself more fully to your work. The point is that if we "look and listen" when confronted with life's roadblocks, we may find that what first appeared to be an obstacle in our path is actually a friendly sign pointing us in the direction we need to go.[4]

In Sum

There was a time when Catholics as a whole were more resistant than other groups to marital breakdown. No longer. Remarriage after divorce may be less prevalent among Catholics than it is among non-Catholics, but the rate of first-time failure is about the same. By and large, the members of our Church are not as interested as they once were in the extraordinary sources of strength that an extraordinary faith has to offer. They think they are serious about making their marriage work, but how serious can they be when they go on ignoring the critical dimension of spirituality? How serious can they be if they are not interested in learning more about their faith and practicing it with sufficient fervor to sail in calmness over a very troubled sea? If only they knew that God stands ready at all times to change the water of their everyday existence into the fine wine of lifelong love and devotion!

Over a thousand years ago, a wise monk named Benedict condensed almost all of this into a single paragraph, one that is worth committing to memory:

---

[4] The Catechism makes it clear that children are not something owed to a couple by God, but rather a gift (no. 2378).

There is a good zeal that can lead a married couple to God and to everlasting life. Practice this zeal, then, with most fervent love. Be the first to show respect. Support with patience one another's weaknesses, whether they be of body or of character. Compete with one another in showing mutual obedience. Do what you consider useful for each other rather than what is useful for yourself. Love one another with sincere affection, and have a loving fear of God. Prefer nothing whatever to Christ.

⤜ Chapter 5 ⤛
Catholic Sexual Ethics

We have reserved our discussion of the physiological side of marriage until now because physical gratification is not only less important than other elements of the marital picture (such as good communication and a healthy relationship with God); it *presupposes* them. Much fuss is made by so-called "experts" about what happens, or fails to happen, in the bedroom. But such talk may be taken with a grain of salt. In many instances, sex has been oversold.

This is not to deny that lovemaking is a good thing, indeed a glorious thing. Despite what critics say, the Catholic Church does not regard the body as evil. Isolated figures within the Church may have expressed themselves in this way on occasion, but not the Church as a whole. On the contrary, it has defended the pro-creative act as something distinctly positive and holy. Granted, the Holy See maintains its teaching that, of all human appetites, the sexual drive is unique in the degree to which it must be brought under control if it is to be man's servant rather than his master. And this is so because marital intercourse, unlike eating and drinking, is potentially reproductive and, therefore, attended with consequences calling for a mature exercise of responsibility. Nevertheless, there is nothing here to suggest inhibition.

The Church is not so much "puritanical" as simply con-cerned—and with good reason. Owing to the lofty purpose for which the marital act was intended, sexual license amounts to a form of sacrilege, and the manifold abuses to which it leads have been roundly condemned: fornication (premarital sex), adultery (extra-marital affairs), masturbation (private or between spouses), incest, homosexual acts, bestiality, artificial birth control, and pornography, to name but a few.[1] Lust of any kind is enormously destructive since it strikes at the very core of a person and, as such, throws his or her entire life, along with that of others, into disarray.

Sex Is About Babies

God engineered things in such a way that physical interaction between man and woman would result in new life. In addition, Adam and Eve were specifically *commanded* to multiply (cf. Gen. 1:28), just as they were warned, after committing original sin, that childbirth would be painful and that they would have to live by the sweat of their brow. Remarkably little has changed over the years. Ten to fifteen percent of all couples find that they are unable to conceive, and among the remainder there are intrinsic factors that in most cases militate against a steady stream of children arriving at regular intervals. Nevertheless, one may be fairly certain of a pro-life mentality in heaven, judging from the nature of the sexual appetite and the length of the childbearing period in a woman's life.

The Catholic idea of procreation, which is founded on natural law in consonance with God's sovereign majesty and Mary's magnificent response to the angel Gabriel, is that all children are a gift from God, whether they be many in number or few, and one must not place barriers in the way of God's generosity. Every marital act must remain open to the transmission of life.[2]

Many who defend contraception in the form of condoms, the pill, and sterilization do so on the ground that its practitioners have a worthy end in view. But such reasoning violates a cardinal

---

[1] See quotations in Appendix B. According to the Catechism, nos. 1755 and 2352-53, fornication is "always wrong" and "gravely contrary to the dignity of persons," while masturbation is "an intrinsically and gravely disordered action."

[2] Catechism, no. 2366. The Catechism goes on to say that "Sacred Scripture and the Church's traditional practice see in *large families* a sign of God's blessing and the parents' generosity" (no. 2373, original emphasis).

tenet of the moral law: namely that one may never commit an intrinsically evil act—in this case, frustration of God's will and the natural law—in order to do good. One may not steal, for instance, in order to put a needy child through college. If and when the marriage act is performed, it must be performed in its full integrity so that the gift of self is complete, and it is only complete when its procreative, as well as its unitive, function remains intact. Only when both parties are consciously prepared to give themselves totally to one another can they attain the stature to which they have been called by God.[3]

Is there not logic in the Church's belief that as God's children created in His image we should be governed by His rules? We may think that a second, third, or fourth child has no place in our lives because the rest of the family would be denied certain benefits. Yet, this is not the way God sees it. From time immemorial, He has sent the most tender of babes into war zones, droughts, floods, epidemics, and famines. Why? Does the Parent of parents play favorites? Or is it because pain and sacrifice, when accepted in a spirit of steadfast faith and loyalty, can generate enormous redemptive power?

Interestingly enough, it is only in recent years, beginning with the 1960s, that Church officials have come under mounting pressure to endorse artificial birth control, for reasons with which we are all familiar. The rate of infant mortality is falling even as life expectancy for adults continues to rise. More and more people have gravitated to urban areas where recreational space is limited. Employees are frequently required to travel far from home, urban housing units are often cramped and small, and the only recognition accorded the ideal of family life is a meager tax deduction for dependents. Many more women are working outside the home at a time when contraception is perceived by many as a safe and reli-

---

[3] Catechism, nos. 2366-67. In the words of Pope John Paul II, in his *Letter to Families* (1994), the "total gift of self to the other involves a potential openness to procreation" (no. 12).

able method of family planning. Finally, from a more general standpoint, history indicates that a nation's moral fiber may be eroded by prolonged intervals of peace and prosperity.

Just as striking, though, is the fact that the Catholic Church, *as a Church*, has adhered so firmly to its traditional teaching on contraception. Confirmed by Pope Paul VI in his encyclical *Humanae Vitae* and soon thereafter by the American bishops' pastoral *To Live in Jesus Christ* (1976), it was reaffirmed by a synod of bishops held in Rome in 1980 and repeated many times over by Pope John Paul II, notably in his apostolic exhortation *Familiaris Consortio.* Dissident theologians who suggest that this traditional teaching must change with the times are flying in the face of an infallible teaching authority given by Christ to Peter, the rock. Over a span of two thousand years, no pope has ever had to retract a single position that he or one of his predecessors set forth in the realm of faith and morals—something of a miracle since there have been a number of popes whose personal lives were far from edifying.[4]

Granted, the Church has altered its requirements on fasting and abstinence, along with mixed marriage. Meat may now be eaten on Friday if some other way can be found of observing the spirit of the day on which Our Lord suffered and died. Likewise, in a mixed marriage, the Catholic party is no longer required to promise in writing that he or she will do everything possible to raise the children as Catholics. Such promises may be verbal. But there is a difference between disciplinary matters subject to administrative fiat and the great body of doctrine known as the deposit of faith (cf. Catechism, no. 84). Basically, it comes down to a question of essentials versus non-essentials as well as the principle that some things will always be wrong. The Church, for example, will *never* approve of murder, suicide, fornication, or adultery. For more on contraception, see Appendix K.

---

[4] See Appendix A on the papacy.

Every Child Is a Gift from God

The celebrated author and convert to Catholicism, G.K. Chesterton, once quipped that birth control, referring to contraceptive methods, meant "no birth and no control." Whether one is amused or annoyed by the witticism will depend upon one's spiritual orientation, what one thinks of the act designed by God to transmit human life, and what value one places on the soul that is being preconceptually aborted.

In this modern, mechanized age of ours, children may appear to be less of an asset than they once were, especially for families struggling to make ends meet. This, however, does not diminish their value, each of whom comes out of God's workshop with an immortal soul capable of giving great glory to its Creator. We all have an instinctive fear of deprivation. It goes with the territory. Yet when we reach deep down into our hearts, we also realize that we do not live by bread alone. As Christians, we have the example of our Redeemer, who identified with the underprivileged by living a life of poverty and who taught that the poor are specially "blessed."

Adversity and hard times are not what one generally prays for. But the record of history, along with our own experience, tells us that there is no situation in life that cannot lead to greatness. If one were to eliminate all those born into families of ten children or more, we would have to do without Thomas Jefferson, James Madison, Daniel Webster, Harriet Beecher Stowe, Saint Rose of Lima, Washington Irving, Franz Schubert, Saint Ignatius (last of thirteen), John Marshall (greatest of all U.S. chief justices and one of fifteen children), Benjamin Franklin (one of seventeen), Enrico Caruso (eighteenth in a family of twenty-one), and Catherine of Siena (twenty-fourth of twenty-five). The roster of men and women who lost one or both parents at an early age contains still another honor roll. Robert E. Lee, one of the most gifted Civil War generals, was only five when his father walked out of his life, never to return. Prize-winning Russian novelist Alexander

Solzhenitsyn never knew his father, and Confucius of China was an orphan from practically the day he was born.[5]

Obviously, no one is obliged to go out of his or her way to have a large family, even though sociologists tell us that such families tend to be closely knit with parents who are confident, accomplished, and devoted. Nor is anyone obliged to have recourse to a fertility clinic where procedures can be as frustrating as they are intrusive.

On the other hand, based on our belief that God loves all His children equally and that He is not in the business of making mistakes, there is only one logical conclusion to be drawn. As soon as one begins to impugn His generosity by assuming that a child born in affluence is a gift, as compared with one born in difficult circumstances (presumably a curse), one ceases to have a fully Christian outlook.

The Myth of Overpopulation

How easy it is to succumb to the notion of "people as pollution." Today's media is full of references to "overpopulation," as if our towns and cities were so many tree nurseries or game preserves, as if our children were nothing but costly and time consuming, a risk to the mother's figure and a barrier to intimacy. The mother in St. Louis who bears a fourth or fifth child is supposed to feel guilty for adding to the burden of Calcutta! Even in Calcutta, we know that life among the poorest of the poor is far from insupportable.

Virtually every prediction by population doomsayers since the time of Parson Malthus (1766-1834) has proven false. One of the more recent examples is Paul Ehrlich's *Population Explosion*, published in 1968 and since discredited. A later work, *The Population Bomb*, shows no sign of being any more reliable. No nation, least of all the United States, is running out of land. Ninety-seven percent of America remains undeveloped, with towns, cities, railroads, and

---

[5] For other examples, see Appendix J.

airports occupying a mere three percent. There is no real connection either between population density worldwide and what we call poverty. In the Far East, the most crowded nations are actually the ones that enjoy the highest standard of living— Japan, Taiwan, and Singapore, for example. The population of East Germany under Communist rule was less than that of West Germany. Yet, its standard of living sagged terribly under an alien political-economic system.

Clearly, poverty has more to do with government policy than with procreation. According to Jacqueline Kasun, professor of economics at California State University, Humboldt, world agricultural resources could support twenty-two times as many people using our present methods of farming. Africa alone could feed twice the current world population. The hunger that does exist affects only about two percent of the world's people, and it is generally related to civil war or hard-line Marxist agricultural policies coupled with ineffective distribution.[6]

Different Holy Fathers have repeatedly emphasized that the answer to population pressure is not to turn people away from the table but rather to furnish more food while making it possible for one parent to remain at home. On the latter point, Pope John Paul II cautions:

> Society must be structured in such a way that wives and mothers are *not in practice compelled* to work outside the home and that their families can live and prosper in a dignified way even when they themselves devote their full time to their own family.[7]

One would never know from much of the talk one hears that children have a supernatural birthright, that each one of them

---

[6] *National Catholic Register* (January 3, 1993), 5. For more on the myth of overpopulation, see Appendix I.

[7] Pope John Paul II, Apostolic Exhortation On the Role of the Christian Family in the Modern World *Familiaris Consortio* (1981), no. 23, original emphasis.

comes into the world with a ready-made passport to heaven. Surely, it is one of today's best-kept secrets that all of God's sons and daughters, whether rich or poor, educated or uneducated, are in full possession of the legacy that such a paternity implies. As Scripture has it, "Let the children come to me" (Mt. 19:14), and "seek first his kingdom and his righteousness, and all these things shall be yours as well" (Mt. 6:33).

This, of course, is the spiritual side of the equation. Nonetheless, it is vital. Without wishing to lose sight of the fact that health, housing, and education are undeniable needs, and costly ones as well, we must never forget that man is more than flesh and blood. He is primarily spiritual in nature, and his spiritual impulses cry out the loudest for expression. Living one's life in accord with God's commandments is not always easy. But it is essential that we guard against allowing material considerations to override the supernatural imperative which permeates our inmost being and holds the key to our destiny.

We hear much nowadays about "quality of life." Note that the word "quality" is defined in such a way that immortal souls created by God for His greater glory count for nothing unless they are well provided for here on earth. Can't you just hear Satan chortling?

The irony is that suicide rates, always a telling indicator of desperation, are highest among the rich. Have you ever stopped to ask yourself why, among permanently crippled paraplegics, the suicide rate is practically zero? Or why, in God's scheme of things, happiness turns up in the most unexpected places? Why is it that facial expressions among inhabitants of the least affluent nations are every bit as bright, perhaps brighter, than those of America's favored rich? Pay a visit some day to one of the "less fortunate" countries of our hemisphere, and you will find crime rates disproportionately low. Pope John Paul II pointed out that our society is "awash in consumerism," and the more one ponders his words, the more one realizes that generosity in procreation is not only a sign of our love, but also a clear witness to the trust we place in divine providence. Is there a price to be paid? Yes. And the same may be said for any worthwhile endeavor.

A Sense of Piety

Most of us would agree that there are certain things in life that one will refrain from doing simply as a matter of form. If an older child sucks his thumb in public, Mom and Dad can disapprove without having to adduce fifty-nine reasons. Likewise, if a person comes to Sunday Mass clad in an undershirt and bathing trunks, the priest has a perfect right to object without furnishing arguments capable of overwhelming the intellect of an Einstein. Just as there is a social sense that adds up to good manners, so too, there is a spiritual sense that translates into a profound reverence for human life. If socially disadvantaged children are apt to grow up without a sense of propriety, youngsters who are spiritually deprived, however affluent and well-mannered, are likely to mature without a sense of piety. The point is that those who are truly refined in spirit will sense instinctively that there is "something wrong" with artificial birth control, not to mention *in vitro* fertilization, artificial insemination, and genetic engineering.[8] And if they don't have such a sense, they will at least entertain arguments to this effect.

It should be noted, in addition, that the logic behind contraception can be used to justify masturbation, abortion, mercy killing, and suicide.

---

[8] See Catechism, nos. 2376-78: "Techniques that entail the dissociation of husband and wife, by the intrusion of a person other than the couple (donation of sperm or ovum, surrogate uterus) are gravely immoral. . . . Techniques involving only the married couple (homologous artificial insemination and fertilization) are perhaps less reprehensible, yet remain morally unacceptable. They dissociate the sexual act from the procreative act," and thus entrust "the life and identity of the embryo into the power of doctors and biologists" which, in turn, "establishes the domination of technology over the origin and destiny of the human person . . . contrary to the dignity and equality that must be common to parents and children." All of this is, of course, in line with the idea that children are a gift from God rather than something owed (no. 2378).

Skeptics will argue that frustration of the procreative process is no different morally from the use of earplugs to shut out unwanted noise. But such a comparison does not stand up under close scrutiny. Hearing may be wonderful, but it is not sacred in the sense that it involves the conception of a human soul destined to live forever. Nor does it entail the same kind of direct intervention by God.

For a more detailed treatment of the case that can be made against contraception, see Appendix K.

Natural Family Planning

Let it be said in this connection that the Church has always sanctioned periodic abstinence from marital intercourse for "grave motives."[9] Such reasons could be economic, social, psychological, or medical, such as a serious threat to the life of the mother or child. In years past, the name given to such a practice was "rhythm." Today, however, there is a new Church-approved method called Natural Family Planning (NFP) which, as a means of postponing pregnancy or avoiding it altogether, is more scientific than rhythm. By enabling a couple to identify the fertile period of a woman's monthly cycle with a high degree of accuracy approximately ninety-eight percent of the time, NFP has been adopted by non-Catholics, as well as Catholics, owing to the absence of hazardous side effects.[10]

Cynics, who regard NFP as an inferior form of birth control because it requires abstinence for a week to ten days during the prime time of a woman's cycle, emphasize the element of risk and argue that it must be backed up by abortion.

---

[9] Pope Paul VI, Encyclical On Human Life *Humanae Vitae* (1968), no. 10, official NC News Service translation (Boston: Daughters of St. Paul, 1968), 5.

[10] The ninety-eight to ninety-nine percent success rate of NFP, assuming it is properly practiced, contrasts quite favorably with that of the Pill (ninety-three to ninety-five percent), condoms, diaphragms, cervical caps (ninety-four percent), and spermicides (seventy-four percent). See *Time* (February 26, 1990), 44, for failure rates; see also *Catholic Twin Circle* (February 16, 1992), 19.

Such views are understandable, but they oversimplify a highly complex issue. NFP, to begin with, is not just birth control by another name. It differs substantially from contraception in that it neither frustrates the procreative process directly nor impairs the integrity of sexual intercourse. To put it another way, NFP does not sever the unity between love and life that God so obviously intended for the procreative act. Contracepted intercouse is analogous to masturbation, in that "sexual pleasure is sought outside of 'the sexual relationship which is demanded by the moral order and in which the total meaning of mutual self-giving and human procreation in the context of true love is achieved.'"[11] But apart from the moral issue, the mere fact that NFP entails sacrifice and some degree of risk can lead to a heightening of mutual respect between partners, as well as to increased satisfaction during "safe" periods. It is also less likely than contraception to arouse suspicion on the part of the husband and become a bone of contention between man and woman during the springtime of their union.[12]

There are only two caveats, assuming both parties are willing to practice NFP and abstinence does not become an occasion of sin, particularly the sin of incontinence.[13] The first of these is that NFP, to be effective, presupposes some degree of intelligence coupled with a considerable amount of self-control. Rare is the husband and wife team that can claim total self-possession at all times. Human nature being what it is, there is bound to be a factor of uncertainty. Three out of ten men surveyed in a 1989 nationwide poll conducted by the Diocesan Development Program for Natural Family Planning said they were dissatisfied with NFP's performance in avoiding pregnancy.[14] It thus seems fair to say that if "grave motives" were not mandated in order to

---

[11] Catechism, no. 2352, quoting Congregation for the Doctrine of the Faith, *Persona Humana* (1975), no. 9.

[12] See Appendix K for additional details.

[13] Rev. Herbert Jones, O.F.M., *Moral Theology* (Rockford, IL: TAN Books and Publishers, 1991), 542.

[14] *Our Sunday Visitor* (May 17, 1992), 5.

justify NFP on moral grounds, they would be necessary in a good many cases merely for the system to work. And even here, there is no substitute for total abstinence if the situation involves something as serious as the life of the mother or that of a child in gestation.

The other caveat, mentioned earlier, is that NFP is not permissible for all couples under all circumstances, only for those with reasons that are sufficiently serious. As to what this means in actual practice, one hesitates to speak categorically. Such matters are best resolved in conference with a spiritual director whose judgment one trusts—and trusts not because it is lenient, but rather because it squares with the teaching of the Magisterium. The yearning for a more attractive home or one situated in a more desirable neighborhood would certainly not qualify. Neither would the desire to take a longer vacation or to send one's children to prestigious schools.

Church teaching on contraception is undeniably tough. Often enough, it requires sacrifice, even heroic sacrifice. But this is equally true of the Church's position on the indissolubility of marriage, premarital sex, and homosexuality. Life itself is tough. Nothing worthwhile has ever been accomplished without blood, sweat, and tears. How remarkable that even in our so-called modern age, childbirth is nearly always attended by danger and anxiety. Difficulty alone does not automatically disqualify a course of action or invalidate a teaching. If, on the human level, parental discipline, conjoined with affection, fosters the long-range happiness and well-being of a child, is it not reasonable to view God as a demanding parent whose children benefit from divine discipline?

Catholic doctrine is beautifully in keeping with the whole concept of sex as something sacred, something in which God is uniquely and intimately involved. How can one profess to believe in God and God's fatherhood ("Our Father, who art in heaven") and not have great respect for every act linked with such parenthood? Often, one will hear it said that "I couldn't possibly afford another pregnancy," or "My wife would go insane with another child . . . already we lack sufficient space, privacy, and material comfort." The answer to these objections is that God never places more of a burden on us than we can bear, and bear profitably. Parents of large families will tell you they didn't know how they could ever manage with a third or fourth child until the child in question actually arrived, and . . . they managed! One is reminded of the old Spanish proverb: "Every child comes with its own loaf of bread under its arm."

When all is said and done, there is nothing today's world needs so much as a counter-cultural faith that relies on God's grace and recognizes an authority in the realm of morals that is insulated from politics, popularity contests, and conventional views—an authority backed by God's Holy Spirit and that boasts a record of undeviating adherence to the truth for over two thousand years.

Abortion Is Murder

The Bible furnishes a wealth of quotations on the subject of when human life begins and hence what constitutes murder. Take, for instance, Psalm 71: "From my mother's womb you [God] are my strength."[15] Isaiah, in chapter 49, has the Lord giving him his name and forming him as His servant in the womb of his mother. Saint Paul refers to the Lord as the One "who had set me apart before I was born, and had called me through his grace" (Gal. 1:15-16). The same sentiment appears in Jeremiah (1:4-5). The Gospel describes John the Baptist as so "filled with the Holy Spirit, even from his mother's womb" that he "leaped" at the approach of the pregnant Mary (Lk. 1:15, 44). Add to this the fact that the Fathers of the Church are unanimous in their condemnation of abortion, and there is but one conclusion: the direct killing of a child—any child, at any stage of gestation, and for any reason—is an abomination.

---

[15] New American Bible translation.

There will always be those who claim to know when human life, as compared with fetal life, begins. But this is casuistry. Common sense dictates that a baby who is human at six months is also human at six months minus a day. By the same token, one that is human at three months was human the day before. And so on all the way back to conception.

What we are witnessing today is a holocaust of unprecedented proportions, one which has taken the lives of tens of millions in the United States alone, and which continues unabated in spite of conscience, Sacred Scripture, and the unanimous verdict of the Fathers. Only in a culture of death could ninety-five percent of the abortions be for convenience (with forty percent of them repeat performances by the same mother). Less than five percent involve rape, incest, or danger to the life of the mother.[16]

What many women do not know is that abortion can itself pose a threat to the life of the mother, and if not to her life, then to her general health. Don Feder, in *A Jewish Conservative Looks at Pagan America*,[17] cites a Canadian study of 84,000 teenage abortions that found laceration of the cervix in twelve percent of cases, hemorrhage (8%), infection (7%), and a perforated uterus (4%). Abortion has been known to cause clotting and strokes, and those involved are said to stand a thirty percent greater chance of developing breast cancer.[18] According to Dr. Bernard Nathanson, a convert and former abortionist, the number of serious complications from abortion every year in America alone runs into the thousands.

Emotional disturbances resulting from the killing of an unborn infant include guilt, depression, anger, lowered self-esteem, suicidal urges, emotional numbness, and sexual problems. Anne Speckhard, Ph.D., in her study of postabortion syndrome,

---

[16] *The New York Times* (August 26, 1992), A23.

[17] Don Feder, *A Jewish Conservative Looks at Pagan America* (Lafayette, LA: Huntington House Publishers, 1993).

[18] *Ibid.*, 185-86, and *U.S. News & World Report* (November 7, 1994), 70.

has listed, among the more common symptoms, hallucination (23%), perceived visitation from the aborted child (35%), nightmares (54%), feelings of craziness (69%), and preoccupation with the aborted child (81%). Speckhard found further that sixty-one percent of the cases increased their use of alcohol, sixty-five percent had thoughts of suicide, sixty-nine percent were sexually inhibited thereafter, seventy-seven percent experienced difficulty in communication, and eighty-one percent wept frequently.[19]

Abortion rights, once hailed as a weapon in campaigns against illegitimacy, have failed to produce any of the expected benefits. Illegitimacy rates have actually risen, along with the rate of fornication, in the wake of easy access to abortion.[20]

Marital Intercourse

The worst thing that can happen to sex—the surest way to ruin it, in fact—is to place too much of a premium on it. As indicated above, the physical side of lovemaking cannot stand alone. It is unique in its absolute dependence on the proper functioning of other elements. Thus, if husband and wife are psychologically at odds, they are unlikely to find what they are looking for in the marriage bed—not for any length of time, at least.

How often couples should engage in intercourse depends entirely on the situation. Three times a day or three times a year can both be "right," depending on such factors as health, pregnancy, and the pressure of work. No spouse wants to be regarded as an automaton. Besides, true joy tends to catch us unawares at moments we least expect and at times when we are least self-conscious.

Beware of preconceived notions of "compatibility." Sexual gratification often lags behind desire. One or the other partner, or both, may be tired, nervous, or distracted, and such a condition can linger for protracted periods. At times like this, one's

---

[19] Anne Speckhard and Vincent Rue, "Postabortion Syndrome: An Emerging Public Health Concern," *Journal of Social Issues* (Fall 1992), vol. 48, no. 3, 95.
[20] *The Wall Street Journal* (August 9, 1994), A13.

aim should be to express love and tenderness in whatever way is possible. The irony is that the more one forgets about self and concentrates on the "other," the greater the sense of personal fulfillment. Jesus held that to "save" one's life, one must "lose" it, and there is no better example of this than in the mystical relationship we call marriage.

Husbands generally take the lead in lovemaking. But again, there are no hard and fast rules except to say that a considerate partner will not make advances when the other is plainly exhausted or, for any other reason, indisposed. In addition, neither partner should discourage sexual advances without sufficient cause and without assuring his or her mate that intimacy is only a matter of time. One would not want one's mate to feel discouraged or to "give up," so to speak. As Saint Paul put it:

> The husband should give to his wife her conjugal rights, and likewise the wife to her husband. For the wife does not rule over her own body, but the husband does; likewise the husband does not rule over his own body, but the wife does. Do not refuse one another except perhaps by agreement for a season, that you might devote yourselves to prayer; but then come together again, lest Satan tempt you through lack of self-control (1 Cor. 7:3-5).

Naturally, there will be times when one may have to forego union in order to attend to the duties of a well-ordered life. It would be imprudent on a regular basis, for instance, to put one's love ahead of professional or family responsibilities, not to mention one's obligation to God.

It goes without saying, too, that no one is ever obliged to engage in lovemaking that is indecent. Anything that might be offensive to a spirit of moderation, modesty, and refinement is out of the question. One's spouse may never be regarded as the object of lustful desire (GS 51). But having said this, one can be as passionate and uninhibited as one likes as long as both parties feel comfortable and retain their dignity as children of God (cf. 1 Thess. 4:3-5).

One or two other observations will suffice. It is not a good practice to give the impression of desiring physical intimacy unless one is actually prepared to follow through. To lead one's mate on, as it were, would be just as wrong as foisting one's passion on an unsuspecting partner without laying the proper groundwork. However, tokens of affection tendered in the hours and days preceding sexual union, as well as a gradual lead-up to the act itself, can be of great importance, particularly to the woman. Finally, there is a need for both parties to pace themselves so that the "faster" one, usually the man, allows the one who is "slower" to catch up. He must exercise control while she strives to "let go" so as to compensate for a slower pace of arousal.

Why Listen to the Church?

Some of my readers may wonder why something as natural as lovemaking should be the subject of so many rules and regulations. The answer is simple: This is the way God made it. There is a divine instruction manual for every human activity. It is called the Bible. And it is worth consulting. Most of the "rules" are self-evident, and for the rest we can rely on Peter and his successors. All of which brings us full circle to the need for discipline and papal teaching. Anyone who is tempted to doubt the authority of the Catholic Church because it makes greater demands than other churches should remember that Christ Himself took an extremely hard line on many questions. Time and again, He held His disciples to a standard of behavior that can only be described as exacting. Was it not normal for the twelve to be terrified when they were rocked by a storm on the Sea of Galilee? Yet Jesus rebuked them for their lack of trust, exclaiming, "O men of little faith" (Mt. 8:26). When Peter suggested that the Messiah needn't suffer at the hands of His enemies—a human enough sentiment—Our Lord recoiled angrily, calling him "Satan" and bidding him *"Get behind me"* (Mk. 8:33).

Christ's teaching on marriage was so rigid by the standard of the day that it caused His apostles to inquire, "Who, then, should get married?" At which point, instead of qualifying what He had to say, He went a step further and stated a preference for celibacy (Mt. 19:10-12). Again, when one of His followers, who had expressed interest in the ministry, pleaded for permission to attend the funeral of his father before joining the apostolate, the Master would not hear of it: "*Leave the dead to bury their own dead*," he shot back. When another would-be follower asked if he could return home and bid his family farewell before signing on, this too was denied. "No one," replied Jesus, "who puts his hand to the plow and looks back is fit for the kingdom of God" (Lk. 9:60-62).

Our Lord may have been kind and compassionate when dealing with repentant sinners, but He was not easy. The adulteress who escaped death by stoning owing to His timely intervention found herself under a firm injunction: "go, and do not sin again" (Jn. 8:11). This was an individual who taught that it was sinful for a man even to look at a woman with lust, let alone commit adultery. Here was a Savior who warned that the gate to His kingdom was "narrow" and that "few" would enter (Mt. 7:13-14). Jesus denounced whole classes of people as, for example, lawyers, scribes, and Pharisees. He cautioned against riches, declared the poor "blessed," and subjected certain towns to scorching condemnation, among them Capernaum (His headquarters), Corozain, and Bethsaida (home to three of His apostles). Now if Our Lord was so sternly unbending in ways that ran against the grain, and which still do, would He not want His Church to reflect something of this same quality down through the years? From all that we know about life as an endurance test, what reason do we have to expect that eternal happiness can be purchased on the cheap? Just as the ways of God are not the ways of men, neither should one expect the ways of God's holy Church to be the ways of men.

Those who doubt that Christ established a religious organization with genuine authority to bind in matters of faith and morals should consult Sacred Scripture. Hundreds, if not thousands, of first-generation Christians gave their lives for the privilege of testifying to the truth of what this Scripture contains. And they did it within thirty to forty years of Jesus' Crucifixion. Many of them were eyewitnesses of Christ's ministry or, at the very least, acquainted with persons who had walked and talked with Our Lord. Yet none of them, as far as we know, had any difficulty accepting the Resurrection. None denied the existence of an organization divinely vested with power and authority. Christ Himself designated seventy-two disciples (Lk. 10:1) and above them in rank twelve apostles. For the principal position of authority, He chose Peter, and it was to Peter alone that He entrusted the "keys to the kingdom of heaven," to Peter alone that He gave the instruction: "Feed my lambs . . . tend my sheep" (Jn. 21:15-17).[21]

The Role of Conscience

One reason why it is absolutely vital to accept the Holy Father as head of the Church is because individual priests, indeed even groups of bishops, have been known to err. Recall the English bishops at the time of Henry VIII. When Henry filed for divorce from his first wife, Catherine, and sought permission to remarry, the Holy Father responded with a polite but firm refusal. And how did the bishops react? Only one of them risked the ire of the court to side with Rome. Only one joined Sir Thomas More, Henry's chancellor and the second most powerful man in the realm, in a course that led to martyrdom. It is immaterial that Henry executed two wives and married several others. The crux of the issue is that his defiance, linked with the defection of an overwhelming majority of bishops, caused most of England to separate from the Catholic Church.

Some who sided with Henry may have done so in good conscience, but this does not make them any the less wrong.

---

[21] See Appendix A.

Well-meaning individuals commit egregious acts every day out of ignorance. One's conscience is never proof against error unless it is formed in light of what the Holy Father teaches. And thus it is that we are obliged, when in doubt, to be unsparing in our effort to ascertain papal teaching.

Let's face it, truth and justice have never been the path to riches and fame. The Church's teachings will always appear "unrealistic" to men and women of the world. Particularly so today. Ours is a society where generosity in family matters reaps few, if any, rewards. Since many of us find ourselves in a quandary, it may seem naïve, if not suicidal, to embrace Catholic values. But we must not be discouraged. Christ Himself, during His public ministry, convinced relatively few of the truth of His message. Yet, there were those at the time who recognized Him as "the Way, the Truth, and the Life," just as there will always be some wise enough to see that truth does not always coincide with the view of the majority. There were not many then nor are there many today. But those who are brave enough, and sufficiently confident in God's providence, to sacrifice for their ideals will receive grace in abundance. Theirs will be a joy that is deep and lasting in the present world—their yoke will be easy, their burden light—and when the time comes for them to die, they will know that they have run the race and kept the course, and that their Savior has prepared a special place for them in heaven.

Appendix A
The Case for Papal Teaching Authority

The case for papal infallibility, which assumes that a pontiff is speaking as head of the Church (*ex cathedra*) and addressing the Church as a whole on matters of faith and morals, rests to a large degree on Christ's charge to Peter:

> You are Peter, and on this rock I will build my church, and the powers of death shall not prevail against it. I will give you the keys of the kingdom of heaven, and whatever you bind on earth shall be bound in heaven, and whatever you loose on earth shall be loosed in heaven (Mt. 16:18-19).

The Protestant claim that Peter was simply one of the apostles with no special authority is at best strained. Sacred Scripture, as well as Tradition, portrays Peter as unique in many ways. Although Christ gave the power to forgive sins to the twelve as a whole (Jn. 20:19-23), it was to Peter alone that He entrusted the "keys" (Mt. 16:17-19; cf. Is. 22:15-23). Peter is mentioned first in every official list of apostles (Mt. 10:1-4; Mk. 3:16-19; Lk. 6:14-16; Acts 1:13). He is the only one Christ is known to have singled out as a special object of prayer (Lk. 22:32), just as he is the only one whose name was changed by Jesus—from Simon to Peter (meaning "rock"). The change is significant. Peter alone received Christ's commission to "feed my lambs . . . tend my sheep" (Jn. 21:15-17). He alone was instructed to "strengthen your brethren" (Lk. 22:31-32). He and his brother Andrew were also the first to be called to the priesthood (Mk. 1:16-19). Peter was the first to identify Our Lord as the Messiah (Mk. 8:29) and, following the Crucifixion, he was the first of the twelve to enter the empty tomb (Jn. 20:6). Jesus made a point of asking Peter whether he loved Him more than any of the other apostles, and Peter answered in the affirmative (Jn. 21:15). Peter again was the first apostle to see the risen Christ (1 Cor. 15:5).

Our Lord promised His apostles that He would send them the Paraclete, the "Spirit of truth," and that the Holy Spirit would teach them "all the truth" and dwell with them "forever" (Jn. 14:16-17; 16:13). After Jesus ascended into heaven, followed by His sending of the Holy Spirit to strengthen His apostles at Pentecost, it was Peter who decided on the method of choosing a new apostle to replace Judas (Acts 1:15-26). Subsequently, Peter was the first to preach on behalf of the Church (Acts 2:14), the first to take Christianity to the Gentiles (Acts 10), and the first to work a cure. Significantly, he was the only one of the twelve to raise a person from the dead (Acts 9:36-42). His God-given power over illness and disease was such that the sick would wait patiently for his shadow to fall upon them as he passed (Acts 5:12-16), Peter was the only one of the twelve in whose presence a man and a woman were struck dead (Acts 5:1-11). Finally, Peter was the only author of Sacred Scripture ever to pronounce judgment on another such author. In one of his letters, he says that Paul's writings are not only difficult to grasp but likely to confuse those who are either unstable in their faith or lacking in erudition (2 Pet. 3:16).

Peter was consulted on every major issue that arose in the early Church, and in every case it was his judgment that prevailed (see, for example, Acts 1:15-26, 5:29, 15:6-12, and John 21:1-9). The same may be said of each of his successors, the bishops of Rome. True, he "peters out" in the second half of Acts, but the second half is less about Church administration than about Paul's mission to the Gentiles.

Peter established himself at the seat of empire from whence the Church was able to reach out to the rest of the world. One might add that every major nation ever converted to Christianity received the faith from missionaries who were either commissioned by or in communion with Peter and his successors. Then, too, all the ecumenical councils ever held, beginning with the Council of Nicaea in 325 A.D., were either convened by the bishop of Rome or approved by him.

More recently, the Second Vatican Council made it clear in decrees promulgated by Pope Paul VI (Nov. 21, 1964) that:

> The Pope's power of primacy over all remains whole and intact. In virtue of his office, the Roman Pontiff has full, supreme, and universal power over the Church, which he is always free to exercise. . . . Infallibility also resides in the body of bishops, but only when it exercises the supreme teaching authority *with* the Pope.[1]

Vatican II also stated in its *Dogmatic Constitution on the Church* that:

> This loyal submission of the will and intellect must be given in a special way, to the authentic teaching authority of the Roman Pontiff, even when he does not speak *ex cathedra* (LG 26).

Significantly, no pope has ever endorsed any kind of heresy or proclaimed anything in the realm of faith or morals which has had to be retracted. Pope Liberius, whose tenure dates to the fourth century, was imprisoned for two years, threatened with death, and cruelly treated by those who hoped to procure a heretical statement from him. But such a statement was never forthcoming.

Likewise in the case of the sixth-century pope, Vigilius. Vigilius was a heretic before becoming pope, and his accession to the papacy owed much to the baleful influence of Theodora, wife

---

[1] Quotations are taken from an outline of Council documents published by the Bishop of Rockville Centre (New York, 1965), 11-12, 15, 86. Cf. LG 22-23.

of the emperor, who expected him to continue in office as a heretic. Nevertheless, once he occupied the chair of Saint Peter, his views underwent a dramatic change. "Formerly," he wrote, "I spoke wrongly and foolishly. Though unworthy, I am Vicar of Blessed Peter." The reward for Vigilius was ten years of white martyrdom ending in a painful and ignominious death.[2]

---

[2] See Warren H. Carroll, *The Building of Christendom* (Front Royal, VA: Christendom College Press, 1987), 31-33, 168, 172-78.

Appendix B
Biblical Quotations on
Chastity, Courtship, and Marriage

On Purity

"We must not indulge in immorality" (1 Cor. 10:8).

"Every one who looks at a woman lustfully has already committed adultery with her in his heart" (Mt. 5:28).

"Let not sin therefore reign in your mortal bodies, to make you obey their passions" (Rom. 6:12).

"But immorality and all impurity or covetousness must not even be named among you. . . . Let there be no filthiness, nor silly talk, nor levity, which are not fitting" (Eph. 5:3-4).

"The fruit of the Spirit is love, joy, peace, patience, kindness, goodness, faithfulness, gentleness, self-control" (Gal. 5:22-23).

"This is the will of God, your sanctification: that you abstain from immorality; that each one of you know how to control his own body in holiness and honor" (1 Thess. 4:3-4).

"If your right eye causes you to sin, pluck it out. . . . And if your right hand causes you to sin, cut it off and throw it away; it is better that you lose one of your members than that your whole body go into hell" (Mt. 5:29-30).

"Immorality, impurity, passion, evil desire, and covetousness. . . . On account of these the wrath of God is coming" (Col. 3:5-6).

"The lips of a loose woman drip with honey, and her speech is smoother than oil; but in the end she is bitter as wormwood, sharp as a two-edged sword. Her feet go down to death" (Prov. 5:3-5).

Concerning your neighbor's wife: "Do not let her capture you with her eyelashes" (Prov. 6:25).

Advice to men: "Do not go to meet a loose woman, lest you fall into her snares. . . . Do not look around in the streets of a city. . . . Turn away your eyes from a shapely woman, and do not look intently at beauty belonging to another; . . . Never dine with another man's wife . . . lest your heart turn aside to her" (Sir. 9:3, 7-9). "Do you have daughters? Be concerned for their chastity, and do not show yourself too indulgent with them. . . . Do not look upon any one for beauty, and do not sit in the midst of women" (Sir. 7:24, 42:12).

Saint John's Book of Revelation (the Apocalypse) is not long, consisting of only twenty-two short chapters. Yet it speaks of the sin of premarital sex (fornication) no less than nine times and comes out against adultery, harlotry, and prostitution six times. This adds up to fifteen separate references to sexual sin. For additional references, see Ecclesiastes 7:26; Sirach 26:9-12, 15-18; Proverbs 5 (all of it); 6:20-35; 7 (all of it); 22:14; 30:20.

Regarding a Wise Choice of Friends

We are all sinners, and as such we must be merciful toward others, just as God is unfailingly kind and compassionate toward us. He is ever ready to forgive provided we are truly sorry for our offenses and willing to make amends (cf. Lk. 17:3). Thus it is that we are not to judge others (cf. Mt. 7:1 and Lk. 6:37). God alone judges.

None of this, however, should be taken to mean that we are to tolerate behavior that is openly sinful. On the contrary, those among us who sin openly and persistently are to be warned, and if they refuse to heed such a warning, they are to be shunned. Christ Himself said as much (Mt. 18:15-17), and His meaning is crystal clear from the totality of the Gospel message.

To be sure, Christ dined with sinners. But some of them, such as Zacchaeus, for example, were not so much sinners as social outcasts, while others had repented by the time they made contact with Jesus. The principal points to bear in mind with reference to Jesus' public appearances are:

1. He dined as a preacher in His preaching capacity. He was not taking a girlfriend to cocktail hours; and
2. There is no evidence that He engaged in small talk. On the contrary, He is cited as having lectured both host and fellow guests for social lapses (Lk. 14). At one dinner party given by a leading Pharisee, Jesus outraged His host by working a cure on the Sabbath, upbraiding the other guests when they maneuvered for high positions at table, and chiding His host for not inviting a broader cross-section of society. He even hinted that Jews could not count on automatic admission to the dinner party that counted most.

At another banquet, a female penitent bathed His feet with her tears, then wiped them dry with her hair and anointed them with ointment. When the host complained that Jesus was inadvertently accepting the ministrations of a loose woman, Jesus turned on His accuser and rebuked him for ignoring his duty as host: "You gave me no water for my feet. . . . You gave me no kiss. . . . You did not anoint my head with oil" (Lk. 7:36-49).

For additional Scripture passages dealing with Christian behavior toward those who are openly and persistently sinful, see the following:

1. Christ Himself said that if your brother sins, reprimand him; if this does not suffice, do so in the company of others; and if he still persists, "Let him be to you a Gentile or a tax collector" (i.e., shun him). See Matthew 18:15-17 and Titus 3:10.

2. Christ also said that if a town refuses to receive your message, you are to shake the dust of that town from your feet and move on (Lk. 10:10-11). He was not one to suffer fools gladly, nor did He recommend the practice to His disciples.

3. Saint Paul tells us not to socialize or dine with those who are immoral, foul-mouthed, greedy, or drunkards. "Drive out the wicked person from among you," he adds (1 Cor. 5:9-13).

4. "Bad company ruins good morals" (1 Cor. 15:33).

5. "Men will be lovers of self, lovers of money, proud, arrogant . . . ungrateful, unholy, inhuman, implacable, slanderers, profligates, fierce, haters of good. . . . Avoid such people" (2 Tim. 3:2-5).

6. "Take note of those who create dissensions and difficulties, in opposition to the doctrine which you have been taught: avoid them" (Rom. 16:17).

7. "Keep away from any brother who is living in idleness and not in accord with the tradition that you received from us" (2 Thess. 3:6).

8. "As for a man who is factious, after admonishing him once or twice, have nothing more to do with him, knowing that such a person is perverted and sinful" (Tit. 3:10).

9. Paul twice advises his flock to let a curse be upon any preacher who departs from the approved, orthodox line of teaching (cf. Gal. 1:9).

10. John the Evangelist speaks in similar terms: "If anyone comes to you and does not bring this doctrine [i.e. proves to be a heretic], do not receive him . . . for he who greets him shares his wicked work" (2 Jn. 10-11).

11. Old Testament quotations: "Whoever touches pitch will be defiled, and whoever associates with a proud man will become like him" (Sir. 13:1). See also Sirach 12:1-7; 22:12-13; Psalm 15:1-4 ("Despise the reprobate, honor those who fear the Lord"); and Psalm 139:21-22.

12. Saint Anthony of the Desert warned fellow Christians of Alexandria to "have no fellowship with the most impious Arians, for there is no communication between light and darkness . . . creation itself is angry with them."[1]

---

[1] Carroll, *Building of Christendom*, 21.

On the Permanence of Marriage (Indissolubility)

Please note—the quotations that follow are the only ones found in the New Testament on the subject of divorce:

"Every one who divorces his wife and marries another commits adultery, and he who marries a woman divorced from her husband commits adultery" (Lk. 16:18).

"A man shall leave his father and mother and be joined to his wife, and the two shall become one. . . . What therefore God has joined together, let not man put asunder. . . . Whoever divorces his wife and marries another, commits adultery against her; and if she divorces her husband and marries another, she commits adultery" (Mk. 10:7-12).

"Every one who divorces his wife, except on the ground of unchastity, makes her an adulteress; and whoever marries a divorced woman commits adultery" (Mt. 5:32). See also Matthew 19:3-9. Note that although Jesus speaks of a man divorcing his wife on account of "unchastity" (or, in other translations, "immorality"), He does not speak of a man's right to remarry. Instead, He implies that such a right does not exist when He says that a man may not marry a woman who has been divorced. This being so, would it be right for a *woman* to marry a *man* who has been divorced (a possibility raised by Mark)?

"To the married I give charge, not I but the Lord, that the wife should not separate from her husband (but if she does, let her remain single or else be reconciled to her husband)—and that the husband should not divorce his wife" (1 Cor. 7:10-11).

Over the years, some Catholic commentators have taken Matthew's phraseology as a reference to the non-binding nature of premarital sex or incest, while others have viewed it as a reference to adultery, one of the cases for which the Church would allow a temporary separation (Catechism, no. 1649; canons 1151-53). Protestant and Eastern Orthodox theologians, on the other hand, especially those who disagree with the doctrine of indissolubility, view the phrase differently. Quite simply, they see it as an escape clause.

How well does the more indulgent of the two readings stand up under scrutiny? If nothing else, it leaves the word "immorality" open to an uncomfortably wide range of interpretation. Anything from a cutting tongue to chemical abuse could qualify. Many Protestant denominations are also flying in the face of history. If divorce had been obtainable in the early Church, surely one would find reference to it in the work of Mark, Luke, Paul, or one of the Fathers. Such, however, is not the case. Divorce is unheard of. Thirdly, Jesus made Genesis His criterion: "but from the beginning it was not so" (Mt. 19:8), and Adam, as we know, had only one wife.

Still another point to be made regarding Jesus' teaching on divorce, as found in Matthew 19:9-10, is that there were two principal rabbinical schools of thought on the subject in Jesus' time, those of Shammai and Hillel. The former interpreted Deuteronomy 24:1-4 as limiting divorce to situations involving adultery, whereas the latter interpreted "something indecent" (Deut. 24:1) more loosely, so as to permit divorce and remarriage in a variety of circumstances. Presumably, the apostles were familiar with Shammai's line of reasoning. Why, then, did they react with such astonishment when they heard Jesus' teaching? There is only one logical answer: What Jesus had to say was new and different.[2]

---

[2] See Leon J. Suprenant, Jr., "The 'Real Presence' of the Marriage Bond," *Catholic for a Reason: Scripture and the Mystery of the Family of God*, eds. Scott Hahn and Leon J. Suprenant, Jr. (Steubenville, OH: Emmaus Road Publishing, 1998), 240-41.

Approaching the question from a different angle, one finds polygamy in the Old Testament. But no sage, judge, or prophet ever divorced his wife to marry another. Furthermore, God is on record in the Book of Malachi as hating divorce (cf. 2:16). From a purely secular standpoint, remarriage after divorce poses serious problems for children, as well as parents. Noel Coward and Clare Boothe Luce treat such quandaries charmingly in their stage dramas, *Blithe Spirit* and *The Women*, and statistics bear out their message: The breakup rate for remarried divorcées is three or four times higher than it is for couples in their first marriage.[3] Henry VIII, perhaps the best known matrimonial rebounder of all time, wound up executing two of his wives. And who is not familiar with similar, albeit less dramatic cases?

According to a recent survey by researchers at the University of Virginia, seventy-two percent of all divorcées are convinced within two years of marital breakup that their divorce was a mistake.[4] All of which is corroborated by Diane Medved's study, *The Case Against Divorce*, which reported that seventy-five percent of married divorcées do not recommend remarriage to others.[5]

A third work by Judith Wallerstein, a University of California psychologist, found that only ten percent of divorcées felt their life had improved, and many of these suspected they might be on the road to another crash.[6] Again there is corroboration. A *Newsweek* poll published in 1967 found divorced women a sorry lot: One in four had turned to psychotherapy, and their suicide rate was three times above the average.[7]

---

[3] Cormac Burke, *Covenanted Happiness: Love and Commitment in Marriage* (San Francisco: Ignatius Press, 1990), 54.

[4] *National Catholic Register* (May 24, 1992), 5. The percentage for men was also fairly high: sixty-one percent.

[5] Diane Medved, *The Case Against Divorce* (New York: DI Fine, 1989).

[6] Judith Wallerstein, *Second Chances: Men, Women, and Children a Decade After Divorce* (New York: Ticknor & Fields, 1989).

[7] Burke, *Covenanted Happiness: Love and Commitment in Marriage*, 60.

Still other studies have shown that divorce is physically, as well as psychologically, devastating. Not only are the children of divorce more prone to drugs, suicide, crime, and poor grades at school, their parents are more likely to suffer early death from strokes, hypertension, respiratory ailments, and intestinal cancer.[8]

In sum, the Catholic position makes sense on practical, as well as moral and theological, grounds.

On the Relationship Between Husbands and Wives

"Wives, be subject to your husbands. . . . Husbands, love your wives" (Eph. 5:22, 25; Col. 3:18-19; see also 1 Cor. 11:3, 9; and 1 Pet. 3:1-7).

Husbands are to love their wives as they love "their own bodies" and as Christ loves His Church (Eph. 5:25, 28; 1 Pet. 3:7).

In the Garden of Eden, God said, "*It is not good that the man be alone; I will make him a helper fit for him*" (Gen. 2:18). See also Genesis 3:16, referring to husbandly "dominion" over the wife.

---

[8] Yancy, "God is God for You," 2.

⁓ Appendix C ⁓
More on Marriage

Impediments to Marriage

Church law specifies several impediments which render a person incapable of entering a valid marriage, making attempts to marry under such circumstances null and void in the eyes of the Church. Such impediments include insufficient age, pre-existing marriage, closeness of blood relationship, abduction, and a vow of virginity that is public and perpetual (canons 1083-94).

Church law also specifies conditions that may negate matrimonial consent and thus provide grounds for a formal annulment procedure. These conditions include lack of due discretion, psychic incapacity, force or fear, fraud, and error about the person (canons 1095 *et seq.*). This second group of conditions could possibly invalidate a marriage, but not automatically so.

The Pauline Privilege

On the basis of one of the passages in Saint Paul's writings (1 Cor. 7:12-15), the Church reserves the right to dissolve a non-sacramental marriage between two unbaptized persons in accord with certain conditions: (a) there has been a sincere conversion to the Catholic faith by one of the parties, (b) the second party refuses "to cohabitate in peace," and (c) reconciliation appears impossible (see canons 1143-50). In addition, one should note that the Pauline Privilege has been a bit tenuous over the years since there is a certain hesitancy in Christian tradition about interpreting Saint Paul's words to allow for more than separation, which is all that is explicitly granted.[1]

---

[1] See *Jerome Biblical Commentary* (Englewood Cliffs, NJ: Prentice Hall, 1968), 264.

Mother Teresa to Engaged Couples

"You are the future of family life. You are the future of the joy of loving. You are the future of making your life something beautiful for God . . . a pure love. That you love a girl or that you love a boy is beautiful, but don't spoil it, don't destroy it. Keep it pure. Keep your heart virgin. Keep your love virgin so that on the day of your marriage you can give something beautiful to each other . . . the joy of a pure love."

Saint Jane de Chantal and Pope John Paul II On Chastity and Child-Bearing

Saint Jane de Chantal (1572-1641), widowed mother of five, had a married daughter who was tempted to limit her family to four children because she craved the social whirl, dreaded the thought of baby after baby, and was concerned that she wouldn't be able to provide for additional children "according to their station in life." Saint Jane advised her daughter as follows:

> My dearest child, you are too fond of the things of earth. What do you fear? That the number of your children deprive you of the means of educating and settling them in life according to their birth? Apprehend nothing of the kind, I beg you, for that would be wronging the wise providence of Him who gives them to you, and who is sufficiently good and rich to support them, to provide for them as will be expedient for His honor and their salvation. This is all that we should desire for our children, and not aggrandizement in this miserable and fleeting world. Courage, then, my very dear daughter! Receive with love and from the hand of God all the little creatures that He gives you. Take very great care of them. Cherish them tenderly, and rear them entirely in the fear of God, and not in vanity.[2]

Pope John Paul II, addressing participants of a Family Ministry Conference on April 28, 1990, declared that:

---

[2] Wendy Leifeld, *Mothers of the Saints* (Ann Arbor, MI: Servant Publications, 1991), 149-50 (quoting Monsignor Bongaud's biography of Chantal).

If the family is established on a healthy basis, it will find the way to accept children generously as a concrete sign of its love of life and as a clear witness of its trust in divine providence, which never abandons those who entrust themselves to it with active serenity.

This goes especially for young families who, if they are trained in a Christian spirit, will not let themselves be conquered by an unjustified fear of having children, and will find a way to overcome the many groundless and selfish tendencies toward putting off giving birth.

To members of the student group Univ, at about the same time, the Holy Father said:

Tell your boyfriends and girlfriends that they should be proud to live Christian purity, that they should love the wonderful gift of virginity, that they should appreciate increasingly the value of temperance and detachment in a world wedded to consumerism.[3]

Daily Prayer for a Married Couple

Thank you, Lord, for the graces which today you planted deep in our souls through the Sacrament of Matrimony. May these sources of strength and devotion remain always and grow like the mustard seed. Help us to love you by loving each other; to draw closer to you by our closer union; and to use the joys and sorrows of our life together as a means of gaining ever more faith, hope, and charity. O God, you have helped us come together; help us to stay together. With your help we have resolved our differences through ever deeper love and mutual understanding and used each occasion to forge greater unity; with your help, we will continue to turn weakness into strength! May our marriage be fruitful as we labor in the great vineyard of this world; and may we come to our eternal rest through each other, with each other, and in each other. Amen.

---

[3] Reported in *The Wanderer* (May 24, 1990).

⪗ Appendix D ⪘
Holy Communion

On the Eucharist

Apart from Church Tradition, there are several key passages in Scripture which support the Catholic belief in Christ's Real Presence. See Matthew 26:26-28; Luke 22:19-20; and Mark 14:22-25. See also the passage in which Jesus explains the Real Presence to His scandalized followers: John 6:1-13, 48-67. Saint Paul speaks of receiving the "Body of Christ" worthily (1 Cor. 10:16, 11:24-29). We also have the testimony of Saint Ignatius of Antioch (107 A.D.): "The Eucharist is the Flesh of our Savior Jesus Christ." Likewise, Saint Justin, writing in 145 A.D.: "The Eucharist . . . is both the Flesh and the Blood of Jesus."

On Daily Communion

Pope Pius X (1903-14) was the first pontiff to recommend this practice for all the faithful, barring serious inconvenience. For his text, he chose the words of the Our Father: "Give us this day our daily bread." According to the Catechism, "the Church strongly encourages the faithful to receive the holy Eucharist on Sundays and feast days, or more often still, *even daily*" (no. 1389, emphasis added).

Proper Dress for Church

The wearing of one's "Sunday best" is as natural as it is becoming to those who join in divine worship. The Lord went to great lengths in the Old Testament to specify that Temple appointments, furnishings, and decorations should be made of the very finest materials (such as gold, precious gems, and rare woods). See Exodus 25-28; Psalm 29:2; and Psalm 96:9 ("Worship the Lord in holy attire").[1] Clearly, He wanted a certain atmosphere. The Catechism says that our clothing at Mass should reflect "the respect, solemnity, and joy" that comes with receiving Our Lord in Holy Communion (no. 1387).

---

[1] St. Joseph Edition, New American Bible.

~ Appendix E ~
Penance or the Sacrament of Reconciliation

Scriptural Basis

Christ forgave sins (Lk. 5:18-24) and passed this power on to Peter, who was to act as His representative: "Whatever you bind on earth shall be bound in heaven, and whatever you loose on earth shall be loosed in heaven" (Mt. 16:19). Jesus also gave the power of absolution to the apostles as a whole: "If you forgive the sins of any, they are forgiven; if you retain the sins of any, they are retained" (Jn. 20:23). We also have the testimony of two saints, James and John: "Confess your sins to one another" (Jas. 5:16; cf. 1 Jn. 1:8-9).

What Is Sin?

Very simply, sin is an offense against God. Sins may be minor (venial) or major (mortal). While we are *obliged* to confess all mortal sins, we are urged to do the same with venial sins insofar as we are aware of them. Three conditions are required for a sin to be mortal:

1. The offense must be serious;
2. We must be fully aware of its gravity; and
3. There must be full consent of the will (Catechism, nos. 1857-60).

If any one of these conditions is missing, the sin in question is venial:

> One commits *venial sin* when, in a less serious matter, he does not observe the standard prescribed by the moral law, or when he disobeys the moral law in a grave matter, but without full knowledge or without complete consent (Catechism, no. 1862, original emphasis).

Examples of Serious Sin

Mortal sins would include serious offenses against the Ten Commandments or any of the seven capital sins:

Ten Commandments
Exodus 20:7-17

1. "I am the Lord your God, . . . you shall have no other gods before me" [such as money, sex, or worldly success];
2. "You shall not take the name of the Lord your God in vain" [no swearing];
3. "Remember the sabbath day, to keep it holy" [by attending Mass on Sunday or late Saturday and trying as much as possible to avoid working on Sunday];
4. "Honor your father and your mother";
5. "You shall not kill" [another human being except in legitimate defense];
6. "You shall not commit adultery";
7. "You shall not steal";
8. "You shall not bear false witness against your neighbor";
9. "You shall not covet your neighbor's wife";
10. "You shall not covet . . . anything that is your neighbor's."

The Seven Capital Sins

1. Pride
2. Covetousness
3. Lust
4. Anger
5. Gluttony
6. Envy
7. Sloth

Examination of Conscience

It is often helpful to think in terms of what we might have done to please God and didn't. In other words, we should confess not only the things we *did* to offend God, but also things we *did not* do that we might have done had we been more considerate or less preoccupied with self (see also Catechism, no. 1454).

What One Says to the Priest in Confession

To begin: "Bless me father, for I have sinned. It has been three weeks (or whatever period) since my last Confession. Since that time, I have . . . " (list the sins you have committed and for each one the approximate number of times).

To conclude: (after the priest gives you your penance), say the Act of Contrition: "O my God, I am heartily sorry for having offended Thee, and I detest all my sins because I dread the loss of heaven and the pains of hell. But most of all because I offend Thee, my God, who art all good and deserving of all my love. I firmly resolve, with the help of Thy grace, to confess my sins, to do penance, and to amend my life. Amen."

To Receive Communion

Saint Paul warns that he who consumes the host or drinks the cup of the Lord unworthily "will be guilty of profaning the body and blood of the Lord" (1 Cor. 11:27). In order to receive the Eucharist worthily, we must confess all mortal sins committed since our last Confession. Naturally, we will feel closer to God and, therefore, make a better approach to Communion, if we confess on a regular basis such as once every three weeks.

Opportunities for Mass and Confession

There can be little excuse for not receiving the sacraments regularly. The Church goes out of its way to make them available, particularly in large cities. Take, for example, New York, where St. Jean's Church (Lexington and 76th Street) has daily Mass at 6:15, 7, 7:30, 8, 9, 12:10, 1, 5:30, and 7:30, while Confessions are heard every day from 11:40 to 12:10, 4 to 5:30, and 7 to 7:30. St. Agnes Church (between Lexington and Third Avenue at 43rd Street) offers Masses every half hour from 7 to 9 a.m. as well as at mid-day and during the late afternoon. Confessions are heard at all of the same times. What an extraordinary opportunity, and still another reason to be a Catholic!

Check the schedule of churches nearest you. An excellent resource in this regard is www.masstimes.com.

Appendix F
Bearing Witness

Saint Peter wrote: "Always be prepared to make a defense to anyone who calls you to account for the hope that is in you" (1 Pet. 3:15). Jesus told His disciples, and He was speaking to us as well:

> Have no fear of them. . . . What I tell you in the dark, utter in the light; and what you hear whispered, proclaim upon the housetops. . . . Everyone who acknowledges me before men, I also will acknowledge before my Father who is in heaven; but whoever denies me before men, I also will deny before my Father who is in heaven (Mt. 10:26-33).

The Second Vatican Council declared that:

> The laity are to be specially trained in dialogue [on the subject of religion] with others. . . . The true apostle is on the lookout for occasions of announcing Christ by word, either to unbelievers to draw them towards the faith or to the faithful to instruct them, strengthen them, [and] invite them to a more fervent life (AA 6, 31).

⤳ Appendix G ⤳
Heaven and Hell in the Bible

Heaven

"No eye has seen, nor ear heard, nor the heart of man conceived what God has prepared for those who love Him" (1 Cor. 2:9). Jesus spoke of heaven as "Paradise" (Lk. 23:43). He also said that each child has its own angel in heaven (Mt. 18:10). Hence the beautiful children's prayer: "Angel of God, my guardian dear, to whom God's love commits me here, ever this day be at my side, to light and guard, to rule and guide."

Heaven Compared with Hell

Jesus said, "The Son of man will send his angels, and they will gather out of his kingdom all causes of sin and all evildoers, and throw them into the furnace of fire; there men will weep and gnash their teeth. Then the righteous will shine like the sun in the kingdom of their Father" (Mt. 13:41-43). He also referred to heaven as eternal life and to hell as eternal punishment (Mt. 25:41-46).

Hell

Jesus described the fire of hell as "unquenchable" and "eternal" (Mt. 3:12 and 25:41). He spoke of hell in terms of darkness (Mt. 8:12). He said that good and evil would be separated on the day of judgment as a farmer separates wheat from the chaff (Mt. 13:30); and He stressed that the gate to eternal life was narrow and the road difficult with "few" entering, whereas the gate to hell was wide and the road easy (with "many" going that way). See Matthew 7:13-14. On one occasion, He told the Pharisees that they were a "brood of vipers" bound for hell: "*How,*" He queried, "*can you flee from the judgment of Gehenna?*"—Gehenna was Jerusalem's smoldering garbage dump (cf. Mt. 23:33, NAB).

On another occasion, Jesus said that on the day of judgment we would be held accountable not only for deliberate sin, but for every idle word we utter (Mt. 12:36). Jesus let it be known that an entire town, Capernaum, would be condemned to hell for its iniquitous behavior (Mt. 11:20-24). And once, after Our Lord cured a paralytic, He cautioned him, "Sin no more, that nothing worse befall you" (Jn. 5:1-15). See also Luke 16:19-26 for the parable about Lazarus and the rich man and Christ's reference to a fixed abyss between heaven and hell.

Appendix H
Scriptural Basis for the Other Sacraments

Anointing of the Sick[1]

James 5:14-16: "Is any among you sick? Let him call for the elders of the church, and let them pray over him, anointing him with oil in the name of the Lord; and the prayer of faith will save the sick man, and the Lord will raise him up; and if he has committed sins, he will be forgiven." See also Mark 6:13: "they cast out many demons, and anointed with oil many that were sick and healed them."

Baptism

Jesus said: "Go therefore and make disciples of all nations, baptizing them in the name of the Father and of the Son and of the Holy Spirit" (Mt. 28:19). He also told Nicodemus, "Truly, truly, I say to you, unless one is born of water and the Spirit, he cannot enter the kingdom of God" (Jn. 3:5). Jesus Himself was, of course, baptized by John the Baptist in the Jordan River.[2]

Confirmation

See Acts 8:14-17, as well as Catechism, nos. 1285-1321, and scriptural passages therein. On being a "soldier of Christ," see Ephesians 6:13-17.

---

[1] Formerly known as Extreme Unction.
[2] See generally, Kimberly Hahn, "Born Again: What the Bible Teaches About Baptism," *Catholic for a Reason: Scripture and the Mystery of the Family of God*, eds. Scott Hahn and Leon J. Suprenant, Jr. (Steubenville, OH: Emmaus Road Publishing, 1998), 113-38.

⁀ Appendix I ⁀
More on the Myth of Overpopulation

Anyone seriously interested in the question of population should read such respected economists as Julian Simon, author of *Population Matters*, and Jacqueline Kasun, author of *The War Against Population*.[1]

Contrary to what one would gather from the media, air pollution and other environmental hazards have become less, rather than more, severe in certain areas. Los Angeles, for example, has made notable advances in improving the quality of its air, especially in the thirty-five years since it came to be known as "Smog City."

The world's supply of natural resources, again contrary to expectation, has more than kept pace with rising birthrates. Interestingly enough, the price of many vital commodities such as oil, electricity, and natural gas has actually declined over the years. Copper, nickel, chrome, tin, and tungsten are all cheaper than they once were, giving the lie to one of Erlich's better known theories. At the same time, many of yesterday's so-called "essential" resources such as whale oil and coal are no longer essential thanks to a variety of technological breakthroughs. Natural gas alone is estimated to be in large enough supply to last 1,000 to 2,500 years.

When it comes to food, the outlook is again encouraging. A good many developing countries (33, according to *The New York Times*) have realized more than enough gains in agricultural productivity to sustain a burgeoning populace. During the period 1970 to 1985, the percentage of people living in poverty in developing countries fell from 52 to 44 percent. Meanwhile, here

---

[1] Julian Simon, *Population Matters: People, Resources, Environment, and Immigration* (New Brunswick, NJ: Transaction Publishers, 1990). Jacqueline Kasun, *The War Against Population: The Economics and Ideology of Population Control* (San Francisco: Ignatius Press, 1988).

at home, the United States' labor force is expected to remain steady over the next thirty years.[2]

On the personal level, if Catholic leaders have been more insistent than most about bringing additional food to the table in lieu of turning people away, they are not alone. In countries such as Egypt and Iran, religious values similar to our own have acted as a formidable barrier to the introduction of artificial birth control. Faithful Moslems and devout Hindus believe that every child is a gift from God. The celebrated Indian nationalist, Mahatma Gandhi, preached that marital union without the desire for progeny is a crime.

Scientific research, funded in large part by the Ford and Rockefeller Foundations, has led to the discovery of greatly superior strains of wheat and rice which have revolutionized food production around the world. Before the utilization of new grains such as the IR-S in places like Vietnam, many nations were hard pressed to meet their domestic needs. Today, these same countries find themselves in the export business. Improvements in well-digging, fertilizers, and the use of polyethylene ditch liners played a major role in India's "Green Revolution," which has caused land values in certain areas to soar as much as six hundred percent in the space of a few years. Here, as elsewhere, the migration of rural people to urban areas was completely reversed.

The United States, which produces more food than it can consume—from the Great Depression of 1929 to 1941, American farmers were paid to plow food under—has long taken upon itself the task of relieving overseas famine, and there is no limit to what can be accomplished provided there is sufficient capital. The point is that one must never underestimate the power of human ingenuity when it comes to devising systems capable of

---

[2] See *The New York Times* (April 30, 1992), A12; Robert J. Hutchinson, "Overpopulation: The Myth That Won't Die," *Catholic Twin Circle* (January 13, 1991), 10-11; see also Barbara Insel's excellent article, "A World Awash in Grain," *Foreign Affairs* (Spring 1985).

sustaining life under the most adverse conditions. Synthetic foods, ocean floor farming, solar energy, and the coming revolution in transport will act to counterbalance whatever pressure may be generated by a rising birthrate.

When all is said and done, Planned Parenthood will go on sponsoring plans for the prevention of parenthood, all in the name of prudence and charity, and it will do so in spite of the fact that the myth of overpopulation is just that, a myth; in spite of the fact that there is no reliable evidence to show that the world is headed for catastrophe; and in spite of the fact that there is no demonstrable link between secular-materialist policies aimed at guaranteeing higher standards of living and that most elusive of all human conditions—happiness. We must therefore be on constant guard against fraudulent claims and false alarms.

≍ Appendix J ≍
Famous Orphans and Children from Large Families

The following individuals were born into families of:

7 children: George Washington, greatest of all American leaders (he also lost his father at age eleven); Saint Thomas Aquinas, greatest of all Church thinkers and writers; and Johann Sebastian Bach, musical composer par excellence (Bach lost his mother when he was only nine, and soon after that his father).

8 children: Charles Dickens (the family was also financially strapped).

9 children: Grover Cleveland, one of the better two-term American presidents (his father died when he was sixteen), and Saint Thérèse of Lisieux. The painter, Rembrandt, was eighth in a family of at least nine children.

10 children: Thomas Jefferson, James Madison, and James Polk (all three were president of the United States). Also Daniel Webster (ninth of ten children) and John C. Calhoun, two of our all-time great senators; John Philip Sousa, America's "march king" and the composer of *Stars and Stripes Forever*; Grandma Moses, most celebrated of American folk painters; and Sir Arthur Conan Doyle, the author of the famous Sherlock Holmes mysteries.

11 children: Washington Irving, one of the greatest of early American writers (while his older brothers went to college, he went to work); also Saint Rose of Lima and Saint Edith Stein. Rose, Stein, and Irving were the *last* of eleven. Finally, Stephen Foster, leading composer of American folk song and ninth oldest in his family ("Old Folks at Home," "Oh! Susannah," "My Old Kentucky Home," and "Old Black Joe"), and Saint Catherine Labouré, foundress of devotion to the Miraculous Medal.

12 children: Harriet Beecher Stowe, author of *Uncle Tom's Cabin*; Franz Schubert, who gave us the "Ave Maria," along with other sublime works of music; and Matt Talbot, "patron saint" of Alcoholics Anonymous.

13 children: Saint Ignatius of Loyola, founder of the Jesuits, was the last of thirteen; also Saint Frances Xavier Cabrini, first American to be canonized.

15 children: John Marshall, greatest chief justice of the United States Supreme Court.

16 children: Henry Clay, one of the best-known early American statesmen (he lost his father at the age of four).

17 children: Benjamin Franklin, most extraordinary of American "Renaissance men," was a scientific genius, savant, writer, diplomat, wit, and practically everything else one can think of.

18 children: Albrecht Dürer, the greatest woodcutter, portraitist, sketcher, and engraver of his age (and perhaps of any age). His family was so poor that his brother Albert had to work four years in a coal mine to put Albrecht through the academy.

21 children: Enrico Caruso, arguably the finest tenor who ever lived, was born eighteenth in a family of twenty-one children.

25 children: Saint Catherine of Siena, twenty-fourth of twenty-five children, was called the greatest woman in Christendom. She died at the early age of thirty-three and has been declared a doctor of the Church.

Among the men and women who lost one or both parents at an early age (in addition to Washington, Cleveland, and Bach) are: Jefferson (at age fourteen), Franklin (who ran away from home), Alexander Hamilton (eleven), Calhoun (fourteen), Jackson, Clay, Lincoln, and Robert E. Lee. Add to the list: Theodore Roosevelt (nineteen), Franklin Roosevelt (a freshman in college), Herbert

Hoover (who lost both of his parents by the time he was eight), Mark Twain (eleven), Andrew Carnegie (nineteen), and Saint John Bosco (Bosco lost his father when he was only two, but his mother never remarried).

In sports, one can name Jackie Robinson, Babe Ruth, and Joe Louis. Foreigners whose names come to mind include Alexander Solzhenitsyn (who lost his father before he was born), Churchill (twenty), Chiang Kai-shek (nine), Confucius (an orphan), Genghis Khan (nine), Stalin (eleven), and Hitler (thirteen)—not all achievers were morally upright!

In the ranks of famous women, one thinks of Maria Comacho, the Mexican martyr who died in 1935 defending her Church with the cry: "*Viva Cristo Rey*" (Long live Christ the King!). Shot at the age of twenty-eight, she was no stranger to suffering. Her mother died when she was a few months old. Subsequently, she lived with her grandmother and father, then with her father and stepmother, then again with her father and grandmother. Edith Stein, martyred in the Dutch holocaust, lost her father at the age of two. Saint Thérèse of Lisieux lost her mother when she was only a toddler, but her father never remarried. Blessed Kateri Tekakwitha lost her mother at the age of four and was raised by fiercely anti-Christian relatives. Finally, Saint Elizabeth Bayley Seton, the first native-born American to be canonized, lost her mother when she was only three.

≈ Appendix K ≈
The Case Against Contraception

The Old Testament contains at least three injunctions to "be fruitful and multiply." Two are addressed to Adam and one to Noah. But the importance that God attaches to human life and the sacredness of the procreative act is even more evident in God's striking down of Onan for a single act of birth control (Gen. 38:9-10). Onan may have been selfish in refusing to raise up issue to the wife of his deceased brother, as later commanded by the Mosaic law. But the swiftness and severity of his punishment suggests retribution for the *way* in which he shirked his duty (i.e., by "wasting his seed"—see Deut. 25:5-10).

In the New Testament, Paul insists on "natural relations" (Rom. 1:26-27), and both he and John prohibit the use of "drugs," variously translated as "secret potions," "sorcery," or "witchcraft" (Gal. 5:20; Rev. 9:21). The Greek rendering of the word is "*pharmakeia*," and it generally referred to the mixing of potions for secret purposes. *Pharmakeia* is never mentioned except in connection with sexual license, and such potions are known to have been mixed in the first century to forestall pregnancy, as well as to terminate it. These facts strongly suggest that the authors were prohibiting both contraception and abortion.[1]

Contraception was also referred to in Christ's day as having resort to "magic" or "sorcery," and again, one can point to evidence of Christian prohibition (Rev. 21:8, 22:15).[2] A real thorn in

---

[1] It should be noted that many popular forms of contraception are in fact "abortifacient," in that they work by causing an aboriton after conception rather than by preventing conception from occurring. See Leon Suprenant, Jr., and Phil Gray, *FAITH FACTS: Answers to Catholic Questions* (Steubenville, OH: Emmaus Road Publishing, 1999), 105-18.

[2] See also John F. Kippley, *Marriage is for Keeps* (Cincinnati, OH: Foundation for the Family, 1994), 78; John A. Hardon, *The Catholic Catechism* (Garden City, NY: Doubleday, 1975), 367.

Peter's side on his visit to Samaria was one Simon Magus, a "sorcerer" or "magician" by Luke's account and the only person denounced to his face as hell-bound by the first pope (Acts 8:20). The closest one comes to Simon Magus is Bar-Jesus, also called Elymas, a name meaning "sorcerer" (or "magician") who practiced his arts on Cyprus, an island known for harlot priestesses and the worship of Venus. And what becomes of Elymas? He is struck blind by Paul for trying to thwart evangelization (Acts 13:4-12).

Scripture must also be read in conjunction with early Christian texts such as the *Didache*, which instructs first-century readers in no uncertain terms: "You shall not use magic. You shall not use drugs. You shall not procure abortion. You shall not destroy a new-born child."[3]

Jesus Himself, in restoring marriage to its original state—as it was "from the beginning"—described husband and wife as "one flesh" (Mt. 19:5), a phrase that can hardly be applied to couples using contraceptive "barriers."

Among the Fathers of the Church, all who refer to abortion, sterilization, and contraception condemn them out of hand, and the list is long. It includes Clement of Alexandria, Lactantius, Chrysostom, Jerome ("Some go so far as to take potions, that they may insure barrenness, and thus murder human beings almost before their conception"), and Augustine ("Cruel lust resorts to such extravagant methods as to use poisonous drugs to secure barrenness; or else, if unsuccessful in this, to destroy the conceived seed").[4]

---

[3] *Didache*, II, 2 (as quoted in Hardon, *The Catholic Catechism*, 367). It should be added that sorcery, which is linked with sexual wantonness and adultery in the Old Testament, carried the death penalty (Is. 57:3; Mal. 3:5; Ex. 22:17).

[4] Clement of Alexandria (in *The Instructor of Children*, 91 A.D.), Lactantius (in *Divine Institutes*, 307 A.D.), Chrysostom (in *Homilies on Matthew* and *Homilies on Romans*, 391 A.D.), Jerome (*Against Jovinian*, no. 49, and *Letter 22*, no. 13, dated 393 and 396 respectively), Augustine (*Marriage and Concupiscence*, book 1, ch. 17 [15]; *Against Faustus*, 400 A.D.; and *The Good Marriage*, 401 A.D.), and Caesarius (*Sermons*, 522 A..D.). For these and other citations, see *This Rock* (January, 1996), 40-42.

The argument is sometimes made that moral precepts, as found in Scripture, must change with changing times. But this renders virtually all of the Gospel null and void. Even if Jesus had never stated that "scripture cannot be broken" (Jn. 10:35) and that "not an iota, not a dot, will pass from the law" (Mt. 5:18), even if Paul had not added that "Jesus Christ is the same yesterday and today and forever" (Heb. 13:8), assuring us that "all scripture is inspired by God and profitable for teaching" (2 Tim. 3:16), and even if Jesus had not appealed to the way things were at the beginning of time (Mt. 19:4), we know that human nature remains constant.

Further, there is legitimate reason to doubt that times have in fact changed when it comes to the fear of childbearing. Ancient fears may have been different from ours, but they were real. The received wisdom is that while children may have been regarded as an asset before the Industrial Revolution, this was no longer so in its aftermath. But where is the evidence? Anti-natalism is mentioned by the Greek Polybius (150 A.D.), by Pliny the Younger (c. 100 A.D.), and by Martin Luther ("Today you find many people who do not want to have children"). Pliny tells us that his was an age "when even one child was thought a burden preventing the rewards of childlessness," and according to the eminent Puritan, Richard Stock (d. 1626), "many men and women, though they desire some children, [do] not [desire] many."[5] All of which makes perfect sense considering that the rate of infant mortality was far higher and child-bearing was attended by far greater risks than now. If children were so widely welcomed and regarded as such a blessing in days of old, why is it that Church Father after Church Father felt it necessary to inveigh against contraception?

Even on the human plane, it is no secret that contraception is hazardous to a woman's health. Barrier methods subject her to a

---

[5] Charles D. Provan, *The Bible and Birth Control* (Monongahela, PA: Zimmer Printing, 1989), 5-6, 34, 50-52, 58, 80-81.

higher risk of preeclampsia during pregnancy, one of the leading causes of morbidity. She also faces intrauterine growth retardation and prenatal mortality. Hormone contraception not only causes blood vessel tumors in the lower coronaries, high blood pressure, and clotting (strokes), but can also lead to bleeding gums, jaundice, baldness, sterility, depression, herpes, loss of libido, visual defects, and problems with breast-feeding.

Intrauterine devices, for their part, tend to cause excessive bleeding, perforation of the uterus, and pelvic inflammatory disease.[6] Women have died from use of the Pill; indeed, they are still dying. It is associated with heart disease and an increase in certain kinds of cancer; and fifty percent abandon it due to a string of unpleasant side effects including irritability, depression, weight gain, and loss of libido.

As in the case of abortion, there are likely to be emotional problems as well. Contraception can be a bone of contention and hence a cause for divorce. Consider the following scenarios: (1) One partner wants to contracept; the other doesn't, and so they argue; (2) He wants to contracept and she agrees, but she fails to follow through properly. He demands an abortion; (3) He wants a child; she has reservations, and nothing comes of their intercourse. He becomes suspicious because she is not opposed to contraception in principle and may be using it surreptitiously; (4) After five years of contraception and saving for their child's Ivy League education, a couple finds they cannot conceive. They are devastated. Fifteen percent of couples are sterile for natural reasons, and contraception can itself be a cause of sterility; (5) After five years of contraception, a child is born, but it is the couple's last, and they desperately want another. One can only imagine how they must feel; and (6) After five years of contraception, a child is born, but it is deformed in body or spirit; and again, it is their last.

---

[6] For more information on this topic, see generally H.P. Dunn, M.D., *The Doctor and Christian Marriage* (New York: Abba House, 1992), 62-70.

Without doubt, children can be a source of discord, as well as a burden, especially if they are not properly managed. But studies show that they are more likely to be the glue that holds a shaky marriage together. Those with large families who welcome children early are less likely to go their separate ways. Many a husband or wife who decided to stay the course "for the sake of the children" is grateful in the long run that he or she did not make any rash decisions.

It is always risky to tamper with the procreative process. Four centuries ago, a French queen by the name of Catherine d'Medici tried to force God's hand. Desperate for heirs to the throne, she put herself under the care of "magicians," and eventually she bore children. But all of them, without exception, came to tragic and premature ends.[7]

With the spread of contraception, sexual intercourse is regarded by many as simply another form of recreation, and with results that are predictable. Among the practices to which separation of the unitive and procreative functions of the marital act leads are masturbation, sodomy, sterilization, and adultery, not to mention premarital sex, abortion, and illegitimacy (how can teenagers be denied the pleasure their parents enjoy if physical satisfaction is the be-all and end-all?)[8]

When Planned Parenthood commissioned a series of studies by Johns Hopkins University in 1971 and 1976 under the auspices of the National Institute of Child Health and Human Development, the findings appeared in a publication of the Alan Guttmacher Institute called *Family Planning Perspectives*, and they were revealing: During the period 1971-76, the number of teenagers in family planning programs quadrupled (from 300,000 to 1,200,000). During the same interval, premarital intercourse was up forty-one percent, premarital pregnancy increased forty-five

[7] Anne Carroll, *Christ the King: Lord of History* (Nokesville, VA: Trinity Communications, 1986), 246.

[8] *The Wall Street Journal* (August 13, 1993), A6.

percent, and the number of illegitimate births rose by eighteen percent. In 1971, thirty-nine percent of teenage out-of-wedlock pregnancies ended in abortion. In 1976, the figure was fifty-one percent. [9] Although one cannot "prove" cause and effect, all of the facts tend to point in one direction.

Pope Paul VI, who condemned contraception in his 1968 encyclical, *Humanae Vitae*, was remarkably prescient. He forecast that artificial birth control would lead to a rise in conjugal infidelity and a general decline in morality. He also foresaw a rapid rise in abortion, the growth of a movement to legalize euthanasia, resort to forcible sterilization by totalitarian governments, and a surge in violence against women. [10] Human bodies, he warned, would be treated as machines—to wit, *in vitro* procedures and surrogate motherhood. Every one of his predictions has come true. [11]

Trial marriage, another product of the Pill-driven revolution, was supposed to afford singles a better chance of finding the right mate. In fact, the divorce rate is fifty to seventy percent *higher* for those who cohabit than it is for couples who live chastely before marriage. [12] During the period 1965 to 1975, which registered a dramatic increase in use of the Pill, divorce rates shot up, doubling and then leveling off in 1975 just when everyone who might conceivably wish to use it was doing so. Again, although a cause and effect relationship cannot be "proven," the Pill's influence on divorce is strongly indicated by the evidence.

Interestingly enough, every one of the Protestant reformers without exception condemned artificial birth control. Similarly, all major religious bodies condemned it until Anglican leaders broke ranks in 1930 and decided to sanction it for "serious reasons." In

---

[9] Dr. Eugene F. Diamond, "Teaching Sex to Children," *Columbia Magazine* (June 1981).

[10] *The Wall Street Journal* (August 13, 1993), A6.

[11] I am indebted for much of the above information to Dr. Janet E. Smith of the University of Dallas, in particular her videotape, "Contraception: Why Not?" (Dayton, OH: One More Soul, 1995).

[12] *The New York Times* (June 9, 1989), A1; *Our Sunday Visitor* (December 27, 1992), 23; *National Catholic Register* (May 7, 1989), 5.

effect, this was a blanket endorsement, for whose reasons are not serious? And since then, the Anglican communion has suffered the sharpest drop-off in membership since its inception under Henry VIII.

To summarize, the Catholic position is firmly grounded in Scripture and Tradition. It recognizes God as a loving, provident Father, and it shields men and women, along with their offspring, from physical and psychological harm. Beyond this, it honors the age-old principle that the end does not justify the means—one may not commit an evil act in order to do good.

≈ Appendix L ≈
More on Annulment

Few developments have done more to undermine the Church's claim to continuity of teaching than the escalating rate of annulments granted by American marriage tribunals in recent years. From a figure of five hundred per annum in 1965, the number jumped to forty-eight thousand in 1981.[1] A nation with only five percent of the world's Catholic population was suddenly granting eighty percent of its annulments. What happened to the Church's traditional ban on remarriage after divorce?

The facts are as follows. The Holy See has always required certain things for a marriage contract to be valid. Underage unions, remarriages, and unions involving kinship of extremely close proximity do not qualify, nor do contracts in which either of the parties lacks adequate knowledge of matrimonial responsibility, full consent of the will, and a certain level of emotional maturity. It goes without saying that in an age when fornication and cohabitation are rife, a great many men and women enter matrimony by the back door, so to speak. Full consent of the will is likely to be missing in certain cases, just as there is bound to be a blurring of judgment when reason takes a back seat to passion. Parental negligence, faulty marriage preparation, and a materialistic ethos have all contributed to this unfortunate situation.

Something else to bear in mind is that while Catholic teaching is divinely inspired, Catholic administration is not. The Church is a human institution with all that this implies. There can be little doubt that annulment tribunals in the world's most permissive nation have erred on the side of overindulgence, and the Holy Father has expressed concern on more than one occasion about the resultant atmosphere of scandal, not to mention the tragic

---

[1] In 1994, the number in the United States was 75,000 (seventy-five percent of the figure worldwide).

consequences affecting children and spouses. Accordingly, Rome has been seeking to eliminate unwarranted annulments by tightening the process whereby they are granted under canon law.

But annulments are *not* divorce, Catholic style. Catholic teaching has *not* changed. Nor can the Holy See be disqualified as the authority on faith and morals simply because some diocesan tribunals appear to be remiss.

One might add that there is nothing automatic about the process. According to recent estimates, only ten to twenty-five percent of Catholics who are civilly divorced have obtained an annulment.[2] Lastly, it should be said that, administrative problems aside, the Church is the only guarantor of truth on matters relating to marriage, and she faithfully proclaims the teaching of Christ.

---

[2] "Reasonable estimates on the percentage of divorced Catholics in America who have received a declaration of nullity range anywhere from five to twenty-five percent. I'll go with ten percent." This is the opinion of canon lawyer and tribunal judge Edward Peters, as stated in "Annulments in America," *Homiletic & Pastoral Review* (November 1996), 62.

≈ Appendix M ≈
Some Useful Organizations, Addresses, and Phone Numbers

1. *Engaged Encounter* (to lay the groundwork for a successful marriage): Consult your local priest or bishop if there is no listing in the local phone directory.

2. *Marriage Encounter* (to make good marriages even better): Consult your local priest or bishop if there is no listing in the local phone directory. Marriage Encounter also has a website that lists local encounters, along with other information: www.wwme.org.

3. *Retrouvaille* (for couples experiencing serious difficulties): National Coordinator: Call (800) 470-2230. International website: www.retrouvaille.org.

4. *The Couple to Couple League* (for couples who wish to learn more about Natural Family Planning and related topics from other couples):

Box 111184
Cincinnati, OH 45211
(513) 471-2000
www.ccli.org

5. ***Catholics United for the Faith*** (operates a toll-free helpline to answer any question about the Catholic faith, and publishes FAITH FACTS on many faith issues, including current information on home school programs):

827 North Fourth Street
Steubenville, OH 43952
(800) 693-2484
www.cuf.org

6. ***Catholic Answers*** (also provides answers to questions concerning the faith and Catholic interpretation of the Bible):

2020 Gillespie Way
El Cajon, CA 92020
(619) 387-7200
www.catholic.org

7. ***Seton Home Study*** (one of a number of excellent home school programs):

Mrs. Mary Kay Clark
1350 Progress Drive
P. O. Box 396
Front Royal, VA 22630

⟡ Questionnaire for Engaged Couples ⟡

What follows is a list of questions aimed at helping engaged parties come to a better understanding of each other. By exploring areas of disagreement, as well as agreement, it is hoped that marriage, when it occurs, will be happier and more secure:

1. Are both of you open to the possibility of having children? Do you know that without such openness you cannot be validly married in the Church?

2. Are you agreed on the extent to which you might wish to be involved in Church-related activities (social, financial, religious, etc.)?

3. Are you agreed on the roles and duties you envision for each other in marriage? Who, in other words, will do what?

4. Are you agreed on basic goals—for instance, the importance you will attach to social status, money, and possessions?

5. Do you feel generally relaxed in the presence of your future spouse? If not, have you been able to identify the source of the anxiety or fear?

6. Are you agreed on how to handle finances—budgeting, checking accounts, credit cards, etc.?

7. Have you discussed how you feel about the celebration of holidays and other special occasions?

8. Are both of you good listeners? If not, have you discussed what you are going to do to improve communication since it is vital for a sound marriage?

9. Do you think you are seeing enough of each other and engaging in enough serious conversation to grow in sensitivity, depth of appreciation, and communication skills? Are you aware that there will be an ongoing need for such time together once you are married? How and when do you plan to make "quality time" available to each other?

10. Are you aware of any personal shortcomings in your partner? Do you understand that they could undermine your chance for a happy marriage? And have you warned your spouse-to-be of what to expect from you along this line?

11. Are you agreed on the kind of wedding you want, how much you wish to spend, and where the money will come from? The burden should not be such that it works a severe strain on either side of the family.

12. Are you prepared to put your eyes, ears, and heart under strict lock and key as a safeguard to marital fidelity, and are you aware that this will entail a measure of self-sacrifice?

13. Have you discussed how you would react to changes in fortune affecting your social status or career that might occur suddenly and unexpectedly?

14. Are you prepared to accept each other as you are, or do you expect your partner to change? Unless you are content with the status quo, you could be headed for difficulties. If something about your partner irritates you, chances are it will be twice as irritating after the wedding. Those who are conscientious will

try hard to please their spouse, but change along this line can be difficult, if not impossible, even with the best of intentions.

15. If your spouse seems pointed in the direction of heavy drinking, gambling, or sexual promiscuity, are you prepared to live with the consequences? Catholic marriage requires nothing less than total commitment under the most difficult circumstances.

16. Are you agreed on the amount of time you would regard as acceptable for the other person to be away with "the boys" or "the girls," with relatives, or on a religious retreat once you are married?

17. Do you share the same views on child-rearing when it comes to discipline, education, and spiritual formation?

18. Are you prepared to accept the fact that your spouse, far from being able to relieve all of your personal problems, hang-ups, and frustrations, may actually add to the burden?

19. Are you aware, as a Catholic contemplating marriage, that your loyalty and determination to go the distance must be such that they will sustain you through any eventuality, including severe illness, paralysis, childlessness, insanity, infidelity, or whatever else may befall you? Do you realize that marriage could prove to be extremely difficult in certain instances and that such difficulty is rarely foreseen?

20. Are you clear on why the Church condemns artificial birth control, sterilization, and abortion? Are you aware, in addition, that Natural Family Planning is permissible only when there are serious reasons for using it? See the section on NFP in chapter 5.

21. If you are marrying a non-Catholic, are you clear on your responsibility to educate all children in the knowledge and practice of your faith? Is the non-Catholic willing to cooperate along this line? And are you aware that anything less than full cooperation could make your task a painful one?

22. If you have been living together with your spouse-to-be, are you aware that this is a serious offense in the eyes of Christ and His Church, that you should go to Confession, call a halt to sexual intercourse, establish separate residences, and do whatever penance is prescribed by the priest?

23. Have you discussed your concept of the role of a "working" mother, as compared with that of the traditional "homemaker," along with the role to be played by the "working" mother's husband?

24. If your spouse-to-be plans to work full-time outside the home, are you prepared to bear the full burden of cooking, cleaning, and child care? If not, what kind of division of labor do you envision?

25. Are you agreed on your priorities regarding child-rearing, community service, work, and personal fulfillment?

26. How do you plan to settle disagreements? Who will be the final arbiter in disputes affecting the well-being of the family after all avenues of compromise are exhausted?

27. Are you prepared to deal with the kind of pressure that may be generated by in-laws? And have you discussed ways of guarding your relationship should it be threatened by such pressure?

28. Do you agree that a loving relationship between you and your spouse should be your first aim in marriage, second only to your relationship with God, and that it should take precedence over the demands of in-laws, friends, associates, careers, and even children, since the ultimate welfare of youngsters depends on the strength and durability of the marriage?

29. Are you clear on the Church's basic teachings? If not, are you prepared to do what is necessary to become better acquainted? Beyond this, are you prepared to share your convictions and religious views with others, a responsibility underscored by Vatican II?

30. If you plan to travel together before marriage without sharing the same bed, are you aware that such proximity, especially if it involves long distances over extended periods, is likely to be an occasion of sin and that it may also give scandal? Do you realize that you have an obligation to care about what other people think and that it is up to you to avoid any course of action that could lead others to sin? You yourself may not be doing anything technically wrong but, as Saint Paul reminds us, there is such a thing as sinning against others by wounding their "conscience when it is weak," and when you do this, "you sin against Christ" (cf. 1 Cor. 8:7-13). We are not even permitted to do what is perfectly legitimate if, in so doing, others will be scandalized or morally weakened (cf. Rom. 14:21). As Christ Himself put it, "Temptations to sin are sure to come, but woe to him by whom they come! It would be better for him if a millstone were hung round his neck and he were cast into the sea"(Lk. 17:1-2; cf. Catechism, nos. 2284-87).

31. Is your relationship based a great deal on feeling, such as physical attraction and romantic excitement, and comparatively little on shared values and goals? If so, you are almost certainly dating the wrong person.

Index

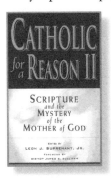